advertising

ON THE

Again, for my family

Advertising
on the
Internet

How to get your
Message across on
the World Wide Web

Neil
Barrett

KOGAN
PAGE

The publication you are reading is protected by copyright law. This means that the publisher could take you and your employer to court and claim heavy legal damages if you make unauthorised photocopies from these pages. Photocopying copyright material without permission is no different from stealing a magazine from a newsagent, only it doesn't seem like theft.

The Copyright Licensing Agency (CLA) is an organisation which issues licences to bring photocopying within the law. It has designed licensing services to cover all kinds of special needs in business, education and government.

If you take photocopies from books, magazines and periodicals at work your employer should be licensed with the CLA. Make sure you are protected by a photocopying licence.

The Copyright Licensing Agency Limited, 90 Tottenham Court Road, London, W1P 0LP. Tel: 0171 436 5931. Fax: 0171 436 3986.

First published in 1997

Kogan Page Limited
120 Pentonville Road
London N1 9JN

British Library Cataloguing in Publication Data

A CIP record for this book is available from the British Library.

ISBN 0 7494 2166 5

Typeset by Kogan Page Ltd
Printed in England by Clays Ltd, St Ives plc

CONTENTS

INTRODUCTION

1

In June 1994, a Phoenix-based law firm posted an innocuous piece of junk mail to around 5000 Internet newsgroups, advertising their services in connection with US immigration law. The response was phenomenal: for the cost of those 5000-odd 'mailers', effectively nothing, Laurence Canter and Martha Siegel received about 20,000 expressions of interest – an unheard-of response rate for essentially untargeted junk mail. They also, however, upset many more newsgroup users and received some 30,000 angry e-mail responses – including death threats – that jammed their Internet account, eventually forcing them off the network. The message was clear: advertising on the Internet is *not welcome*!

In just three short years, however, the position has shifted dramatically: in 1995, the on-line advertising market was worth $37 million; in 1996, US and European businesses spent an estimated $200 million on Internet advertising. Observers such as CyberAtlas, Jupiter Communications and Forrester expect this to pass $1 billion in 1998, and to approach $5 billion by 2000. This is, of course, only a tiny fraction[1] of the current worldwide

---

[1] In 1995, US TV advertising spend was $38 billion and nearly as much for newspaper advertisements. By far the largest spend, however, was on telemarketing, at a staggering $82 billion. In total, the US spend for 1995 was around $240 billion, making the 1996 Internet spend something less than 0.1 per cent of this figure.

market for traditional media advertisements but, clearly, much has changed.

The fundamental shift is that the Internet has become a *commercial* environment. Until 1990, the Internet was owned and operated primarily by the US government, with the main information network – the so-called 'backbone' – belonging to the National Science Foundation (NSF). As a non-profit research organization, their Acceptable Use Policy (AUP) for the Internet explicitly prohibited the transmission of commercial messages across their NSFNET. Effectively, this prohibited *all* commercial Internet traffic, since no transmission could be guaranteed not to use this part of the network.

In the 1990s, however, the US government and the European Union both began eagerly to embrace the prospect of a global information infrastructure, leading in time to a worldwide 'information superhighway' connecting businesses and individuals in a high-speed, interactive 'cyberspace'. This vision called not for *government* expenditure but for the investment of venture capital and commercial sponsorship. As the nearest thing in practice to the superhighway, the Internet therefore began to become steadily more commercialized.

Firstly, the AUP was changed in 1990 so as to prohibit only commercial traffic *issuing* from NSF-funded sites and following this, several hopeful ventures were formed to allow businesses to access the Internet facilities – primarily for the exchange of information related to co-operative projects. In 1991, an alternative to the NSFNET backbone was provided by a group of these service providers. Called 'CIX' (Commercial Internet eXchange), this allowed many more businesses to use the Internet, although again primarily for information exchange between themselves.

Throughout the next few years, commercial use of the facilities expanded and in April 1994 CommerceNet became the first, large-scale implementation of a 'virtual shopping' environment. Individual Internet users could access the electronic shops; this was not for simple business-to-business communication. Advertising outside the 'Internet Mall', however, was still seen as 'beyond the pale' by many.

Because the Internet had been originally developed for and operated by academics, researchers and students, it was of course seen as a medium primarily intended to support the exchange of *information* rather than advertisements. CommerceNet and other 'virtual shopping malls' provided a service, but in what were seen to be distinct and separate areas of the system. When this commercial activity began ever more to impinge on these 'traditional' users – through a series of increasingly unsubtle advertising and 'get rich quick' postings to inappropriate newsgroups, for example – tempers and frustrations mounted. The Internet was being 'abused' and 'polluted': Canter and Siegel's posting was neither the first nor the worst such; it was simply the proverbial last straw.

Between then and now, however, the commercial use of the Internet has exploded. Over 2000 Internet service providers (ISPs) now offer Internet-connectivity to the masses; and those masses are growing rapidly, with projections ranging from 200 million to 1 billion users by the turn of the century. Perhaps the most important change, however, is in the *appearance* of the Internet. Once a strictly ASCII character-based system, the rapid spread of the World Wide Web and of effectively free browser software has created a multimedia, interactive and engaging environment.

As the users have flocked to the network, so too have the *publishers*. On-line newspapers, magazines, and even entirely new kinds of publication have emerged. The costs of electronic publishing are minimal, the audience reach is wide, and the quantity of information that can be offered is effectively unlimited. What is more, the medium allows the newspapers to offer a much *wider* set of information, with cross-links to other articles, other publications and even relevant Web sites of universities, companies or enthusiasts. An on-line news story can be a very rich source of information and can lead the interested reader on into a complex network of related detail.

Electronic versions of well-known traditional-media publications therefore abound. For similar reasons, purely commercial organizations have begun to establish Web-presences, with so-called 'home pages' (explained below) hosted on their own or their ISP's Internet systems. These pages can be used to provide the most basic information about the organization; or can be electronic shopping centres, allowing customers to buy the company's goods on-line; or can be a complex series of engaging, informative and useful elements, attracting and entertaining visitors from a wide variety of backgrounds.

There are now over 500,000 Web sites on the Internet, more than 100,000 of them owned and operated by companies. These corporate Web users are in the main now sitting uncomfortably among the millions of student, academic and research users of the Internet, impatiently waiting for the long-heralded electronic commerce revolution to begin and for those millions of prospective consumers to flood to their on-line stores.

And, of course, there are now the advertisements.

It is interesting to consider the way in which advertising has shifted from unacceptable in the context of newsgroups and mail-lists, to acceptable in the context of published Web pages: this is what I call 'legitimacy of presence' for the advertisement; some advertisements are welcome only within certain contexts, and are unacceptable elsewhere. The shift in acceptability of advertising within the Web is one of the most fascinating and important aspects of the new medium's current rapid development.

Of course there is the consideration that *users* see the advertisements as apparently familiar in nature – a point that we will address in more detail below; there is also the consideration that *publishers*, already used to working with advertisers, have begun to publish on-line material; and there is the consideration that the *advertisers* wish to reach the widest possible range of potential buyers. These are all important points but there is more: although simple, fixed content home pages can be produced cheaply by enthusiasts, it costs a substantial sum of money to establish and to operate a 'professional' Web page containing interesting, relevant and timely content (and content is very much 'king' in the Web): perhaps as much as $1 million for the largest collections; from where do the commercial publishers gain the revenue to *pay* for that development?

The initial experiments in such on-line publishing have been (literally) amateurish, or have been funded from revenue obtained from other sources: a 'traditional' media publication underwriting the costs of the electronic version, for example with the current range of Web-hosted newspapers. In time, of course, these *commercial* publishers will wish to move on to a more commercial footing and to *sell* the access to the material, exactly as they sell access to the publications themselves. This requires mechanisms and processes to support electronic commerce – of whatever description – in the until now anarchic environment of the Internet. Technical and commercial advances, however, mean that on-line publishing and Internet-hosted electronic commerce are rapidly progressing in sophistication and – more importantly – public acceptability. Because of this, it is gradually becoming the case that users can be made (or helped) to pay for the material in question. This direct revenue – equivalent to the payment for a magazine, book or newspaper – will help to fund the Web sites. We will consider this revolution in electronic commerce below.

At present, however, the only source of direct income for these Web sites is from advertising; and the advertisers (for now at least) seem willing to pay for even the most experimental of publishing ventures. As electronic commerce itself comes of age, however, advertising on the Internet will of course change and mature: this book is about the current nature of this advertising, the shifts in electronic commerce that will induce this change, and the eventual future state of advertising itself.

For some of the advertisers the Internet will prove valuable, although perhaps not the gold-mine they first thought. For others, it will be an expensive and perhaps even embarrassing failure. Why will they fail? And how might they have succeeded? That is the subject of this book, which is written primarily to help product and marketing managers of businesses throughout the world benefit from using the World Wide Web to communicate their brand messages, product differentiators and a whole host of advertising messages.

It will also, I trust, be of value to those advertising professionals who would like to know why and how the Internet differs from the more traditional media, of which they have long experience.

And finally, I think that the book will be interesting to those many Internet and World Wide Web users who have become the – sometimes unwilling – audience for increasingly professional advertising messages, and who might feel an urge to understand better the processes and principles supporting those tiny but obtrusive sponsors' logos.

A word of encouragement now to the business and professional reader: this is *not* a technical, computer science textbook; it is not an 'Internet-nerd's handbook'; you need no technological prowess to understand it, although you might well need some to put it into practice. Nor is it, however, a simple business 'how to' book; although I will seek to give you advice, the book is primarily about giving you the *information* on which your strategic decisions for a marketing programme can be built.

The Internet is not a magical tool that will make a poor advertisement excellent, or a bad marketing programme good. You will still need to know how to produce marketing messages, how to target commercials at an appropriate audience, and how to engage an indifferent consumer in a dialogue: I assume that you already know how to do that in the context of traditional media. What this book will show you is how this can be achieved within the global Internet; and what limitations and restrictions, as well as opportunities, the new interactive medium provides.

FOUNDATIONS AND FUNDAMENTALS

2

Before we move on to consider the nature and prospects for advertising in the Internet and World Wide Web, it is perhaps useful to consider some of the fundamentals of that medium. I have assumed only a low level of familiarity with the various concepts involved; those with more experience can safely skip parts or all of this chapter.

THE INTERNET

The Internet was developed by a US government-funded research agency – Advanced Research Projects Agency (ARPA) – nearly 30 years ago. Strictly speaking, the 'Internet' refers to the set of rules (or 'protocols') by which two computer networks can exchange information with one another; it is a lingua franca between different systems. Originally these Internet protocols were used to support the communication between the civilian ARPANET – linking universities and research establishments – and the military MILNET; as connectivity to the ARPANET was increased through the 1980s – and the network evolved into the NFSNET discussed above – the Internet protocols (called 'TCP/IP') became ever more widely used. Interlinked networks running the TCP/IP protocols now straddle the globe, allowing computers to communicate with one another in almost every country of the world.

TCP/IP simply allows computers to *talk* with one another; they must, however, have something to *say* and this is provided by the applications that run on them. In the global Internet there are a set of standard facilities available, from electronic mail, through network news, to remote file transfer. These allow individual users to communicate with one another and to copy useful files of information from remote computer systems to themselves.

Individual users access the global Internet by connecting to an already Internet-connected computer. For university or many commercial users this is straightforward: their computer system is probably already a part of the network; they need simply to log on to it. For other users, particularly the increasing number of home-based users, this involves accessing the computer systems of a commercial access provider – an Internet service provider (ISP). For the most part, this is achieved by using a standard telephone connection and a modem – a simple device that translates the computer-held binary data into a 'tone' that can be played along a telephone line. With this connection in place, they too can access the worldwide collection of information.

Internet addresses

Each computer in the network – sometimes called a 'host' – has a unique address. Like a postal address this has several elements to it:

▶ a *country code*, showing where the host computer is located (such as 'uk', 'fr', 'de');

- ► a *top-level domain*, indicating the type of organization operating the host ('co' or 'com' for commercial, 'org' for non-profit organization, 'ac' or 'edu' for university, etc);

- ► a *domain* name, which is usually the name of the organization that operates the host (eg, 'microsoft', 'netscape', 'yahoo', etc); and

- ► a *hostname*, which is the name by which the host computer itself is known.

There are two peculiarities of the Internet names. Firstly, the Internet is primarily a US-developed infrastructure; by default, the network therefore assumes that *all* hosts are American unless otherwise specified and so there is no country code 'us'. Also, commercial organizations in the US are specified as being part of the 'com' domain; elsewhere, they are specified as part of the 'co' domain. It *is* possible, however, for non-US hosts to register as part of the 'com' domain and so this is not always a good indication of the host's actual, physical location.

The Internet address is then composed of these elements, separated by 'dots'. Hence, my own Internet address is:

uk22p.bull.co.uk

This is an Internet host called 'uk22p', that is owned and operated by the UK-based company Bull Information Systems. Internet electronic mail addresses simply require that the user's login name is written before the Internet address, separated by an @ ('at') symbol. For me, the address is therefore:

n.barrett@uk22p.bull.co.uk

The Internet provides access through e-mail now to millions of individual users, and connectivity to many hundreds of thousands of systems; each one of which might contain seemingly unlimited amounts of useful information. This is, however, fast becoming something of an embarrassment of riches: a growing problem is now the sheer *volume* of information that those systems hold. Finding the required newsgroup article or accessible file can be a difficult and incredibly time-consuming job. Recognizing this problem, in 1990 one of the Internet-connected research establishments developed a sophisticated system to allow students and academic researchers easily to locate information on their system. The establishment was CERN in Switzerland, and the access system has come to be known as the World Wide Web.

THE WORLD WIDE WEB

The World Wide Web is probably the most important part of the Internet – in fact, for many people, it is the *only* part of the Internet that they use; and for some, the terms 'Internet' and 'Web' have become synonymous. It has several elements. Firstly, there is the structure or organization of the computers themselves. This is what is called a 'client–server' arrangement: the computers storing the information are the servers – sometimes also called 'hosts'; the computers accessing the information are the clients. A client makes a simple request for information from a server; the server responds by delivering the information to the client. This is a straightforward transaction – there is no long-lasting session connection between the two.

The second element of the Web is in the organization of the information itself. Web servers hold a set of 'pages', each written in a specific format called HTML (HyperText Markup Language). Each page has an address, called a URL (Uniform Resource Locator). This is made up of the host's Internet address, followed by the location of the file on that server. For example:

www.bull.co.uk/internet/help.html

This specifies a file called 'help.html' that is stored in a directory 'internet' on the Bull Information System World Wide Web server 'www'. Although not all hosts conform to the pattern, the usual form is for Web servers to be called 'www'. There are others – for example, the Netscape home page is called '<u>home</u>.netscape.com'. The '/' symbol is the directory and filename separator on the UNIX operating system. This is the most common Internet host and so the convention is also used within the URLs.

Web browsers

A 'browser' is the software retrieving these HTML pages on the client system – most usually a PC connected via a modem-link to an ISP. The first browser was produced in February 1993 at the National Centre for Supercomputer Applications (NCSA) at the University of Illinois. This was called 'Mosaic' and was offered to interested users free of charge. Browsers became a commercial concern when the original developers of Mosaic left NCSA to establish their own company, Netscape, in March 1994. Their 'Navigator' product is currently the most popular of the browsers, and Netscape is one of the foundation stones of the new Internet structure.

Navigator is not the only Web browser, however. Spry Inc. licensed the sourcecode of Mosaic to produce its own 'Spry Mosaic'. This was in turn licensed by a number of organizations – such as CompuServe as it entered the full Internet market instead of the simple bulletin board service it had offered prior to 1995.

In late 1995, another key player entered the Internet market: after several months of decrying the World Wide Web as a 'playground', Microsoft entered with the zeal of a convert, itself licensing and subsequently extending the Spry Mosaic product. Under the name Internet Explorer, and now a bundled part of new Microsoft operating systems, this is the most serious challenge to Netscape's current dominance.[2]

Accessing Web pages

When a browser requests a page from a given server, the information is passed to it through a specific protocol running over the basic TCP/IP – this is called HTTP (HyperText Transfer Protocol). The contents of the page – that is, the HTML code – are transmitted through the Internet to the client, where the browser reconstructs the page on the user's screen.

Web pages are specified to the browser in one of two ways: either explicitly, by entering the URL directly; or through the process of following a link embedded within a previously retrieved page. URLs are commonly written along with the protocol to be used for retrieving them. Thus, to retrieve the 'help.html' file mentioned above one would enter:

http://www.bull.co.uk/internet/help.html

---

[2] At the time of writing, Netscape are still dominant but with their lead severely reduced. Slightly over 50 per cent of Web accesses are performed using Navigator, while Explorer scores between 40 and 45 per cent. Given the speed at which Microsoft have gained this share, it would be unrealistic to believe that they will not be the dominant player by the end of 1997.

There *are* other protocols that can be specified in place of the 'http', such as 'ftp' (file transfer protocol), but this is the most common within the Web. The '//' is simply used to separate the protocol specification from the host name.

In many cases, the page that is transferred will contain several elements. It might, for example, contain the text of the page along with HTML commands indicating how that text is to be displayed on the screen – called the 'formatting'. The browser will therefore read this set of commands and display the text as requested. Additionally, the page might contain one or more images in standard formats. The HTML instructions will therefore require the browser to request that this 'in-line' image is also transferred to it.

Notice, however, that these two transfers of information are entirely separate: the server system sends only those things that it is asked to send; and the server does not maintain a connection to the client – in effect, the server 'forgets' the client once it has sent the requested information.

As well as one or more images, the page might contain sound files, moving images, even embedded programs (called 'applets') that the browser can execute. In each case, however, the browser must make an additional request to the server for the subsequent information to be transferred. Each request for information is called a 'hit' and can take a significant amount of time to be satisfied if the server is busy, or the intermediate network is overloaded.

Once the total contents of the Web page have been retrieved, the browser's activity has finished and the user is ready to view the page. This might involve reading the text, which could be contained within one or many 'screenfuls'; it might involve playing any retrieved audio or film-clip files, or using the embedded applet. Among the elements transferred to the browser, however, are the hypertext links to other pages which might be held on the same or an entirely different host system.

These links can be simple words such as a company or product name, another user, or anything; or the links might be attached to all or part of an embedded image. The link is activated when the user moves the mouse arrow over it and 'clicks'. At this point, the browser will record the URL to which the link 'points' and will begin the process of retrieving the requested page.

Web sites

Locating information in the increasingly complex jungle of Web pages and disparate hosts can still be difficult. Although the Web makes the process of exploring *known* sites easier, it is still difficult to find which of a huge set of *unknown* sites might be of interest. To help in this, enterprising Web users have established so-called 'search engines': Yahoo!, started by two US students, who sold the company for a large sum of money; Alta Vista, operated by Digital; Excite and many more. Incidentally, these search engine sites are expensive to operate and maintain: they require phenomenally powerful computers, network links and truly immense database facilities. At least part of the funding for these sites therefore comes from the sale of advertising space within search-produced Web pages.

New sites can be discovered by using the large and frequently updated databases held on these search engines. The databases are maintained by a continuous process of exploring new areas of the Web, or by new Web publishers sending information to the database operators. A keyword search in the database is often sufficient to find many thousands of relevant sites, all possibly containing the information of interest to Web users. As well as details of the sites, the engines even retrieve URLs to allow the user easily and quickly to 'go' there.

Web sites can be maintained by a wide range of Internet users:

► *commercial* organizations – to advertise their products, services or achievements;

► *publishers* – to provide on-line versions of magazines or newspapers, or even to provide wholly novel types of electronic text-publications;

► *charities* and non-profit organizations – to deliver information to their supporters or clients;

► *government* organizations – to provide information on new laws, speeches or issues of concern;

► *universities* – to give details on their lecture courses, research papers or as a means of contacting faculty members; or

► *private users* – as so-called 'home pages', allowing them to tell the whole world about their hobbies, political opinions, or even sexual preferences!

The World Wide Web is the ultimate self-publishing (even, self-*publicizing*) environment: a 'do-it-yourself' broadcast media received and operated at negligible cost throughout the world. Amateur Web pages are simple to create, supported easily within the host systems of ISPs or other Internet host operators, and can contain almost unlimited types of graphics, text and 'effects' (sound, moving pictures, applets, frames, etc).

KEY ASPECTS OF THE WEB

By means of hyperlinks and search engines, users can navigate – or 'surf' – through a complex and seemingly endless series of cross-references and links between pages that might be held on servers all around the globe. From the perspective of using the World Wide Web to support advertising, there are several aspects of this description that will prove to be important:

1. most home users are connected from their PC to an ISP account via a telephone line and modem;

2. relevant Web pages are often uncovered by using a 'search engine';

3. a Web page can be any size, from one 'screenful' to many;

4. Web pages can contain a variety of graphics, audio and moving images;

5. a Web page might require several requests to a server ('hits') before it is complete; and

6. the servers do not 'remember' from one browser request to the next.

This is a simple overview of the Internet and World Wide Web technology but it is sufficient to begin to appreciate some of the problems and opportunities that the Web provides. As we proceed, other aspects of the Web will be introduced as required. Currently, the World Wide Web is the fastest growing aspect of the Internet: it is also the element that provides the most obvious support for on-line advertising.

WEB ADVERTISING

3

While there *are* Internet newsgroups dedicated to explicitly commercial messages, by far the most interesting part of the Internet structure for advertisers is the World Wide Web. The multimedia aspect of the Web content is more closely related to the types of advertisements with which they are familiar – such as colour spreads in magazines, boxed advertisements in newspapers and commercial breaks in TV and radio.

More than this, advertisers are used to dealing with newspaper and magazine publishers, and these have both introduced services on the Web. The World Wide Web therefore presents interesting new features – interactivity, for example – but other familiar and comforting aspects that act as an 'anchor'.

The process of advertising products and services is little different on the Internet and Web than it is in the more traditional media: as we have said, the Web does not present a 'royal road' to easy advertising success; the global, interactive facilities of the medium will not make an intrinsically poor advertising concept effective, nor guarantee sales of inappropriate products. The medium *does*, however, have many interesting features that can be used to build a successful campaign.

ADVERTISING

We are all surrounded by a surprisingly vast amount of advertising – so much so, that in many cases it becomes all but invisible – or perhaps, *subliminal*. Advertising comes in many forms: from relatively simple messages proclaiming the advantages or unique aspects of a given product, to complex stories reinforcing the brand image of a well-established favourite. To understand how the Web can be effectively used for advertising, it is of course first necessary to understand what is involved in advertising itself.

The Chambers Twentieth Century Dictionary defines advertising as:

> to draw attention to; to give public information about the merits claimed for

Clearly advertising is about telling the public something about your product. The most important aspect of advertising, however, is often overlooked. Advertising exists for one very simple purpose:

> to increase the number of *sales* of the advertised product by supporting an established, articulated marketing programme

The general public – and indeed, many product and marketing managers themselves – see just the advertising: clever advertising equals increased sales. What this misses is the marketing programme on which the advertising is based; an advertisement that looks 'clever' but which serves no purpose in the overall selling programme is not likely to be successful by the only true, objective measure: increased sales.

Marketing programmes might, for example, determine that a given product could sell more if it was offered at a lower price to a down-market consumer; or it might decide that the target market has begun to overlook the product and needs to be reminded of its existence; or it might decide that the product is perceived as being old-fashioned and therefore requires a change of image, etc. Each of these marketing programmes could well require a corresponding advertising programme, ranging from cheap and cheerful fly-posting, to the most expensive of concept TV commercials. The TV commercial, however, is not necessarily a *better* advertisement than the fly-poster simply because it is more expensive and involves a potentially more far-reaching audience: each marketing programme demands a suitable advertisement appropriate for the *mission*, the *message* and the target *market*.

Marketing programmes revolve around this 'target market': the people to whom the product is *sold*. The basis of good marketing is to understand two essential elements of this target market: who they are; and how they buy. Most marketing programmes will be based on a clearly delineated analysis of the target market, perhaps into age groups, income brackets, geographical location, business sectors, etc. Buying habits might include things like impulse purchases, planned purchases following a specific product analysis programme, replacement purchases and so forth.

Advertising then supports the marketing programme by *influencing* through *impressions* a well defined and *measurably quantifiable* subset of the target market, called an 'audience'.

Advertising audiences

This is that part of the target market that can be expected to experience the advertisement or series of advertisements (a 'schedule'). The nature of the audience mix in terms of demographic, income and other factors is called its 'composition', and its size relative to the target market is referred to as the advertisement's 'reach'.

An advertisement might, for example, be seen by many millions of individuals, none of whom are a part of the target market: its reach is therefore zero and its effectiveness is negligible. Alternatively, it might be seen by *all* of the small number of potential customers for a niche product: its reach is therefore 100 per cent and its effectiveness is determined by the appropriateness of its message.[3]

Advertising impressions

Each time an advertisement is experienced by a member of its audience it is said to have made an *impression*. Impressions must be *effective* and the usual measure of effectiveness is recall: can a member of the advertisement's audience remember the advertisement at some later date?

Some advertisements need to be seen several times before they can be recalled: the number of times an advertisement must be witnessed before it can be recalled to mind is the advertisement's 'effective frequency' – usually between four and seven for most

---

[3] In direct marketing – mailshots, etc – 'reach' is defined slightly differently, as the number of people of households exposed to an advertising schedule. This, however, assumes that the target market is the total population, for example. In this work, we will assume that the target market is a defined subset of the population.

traditional-media advertising. Exceeding this number of exposures is unnecessary and in some cases might even be harmful because the advertisement then simply becomes part of the general background or scenery and is subsequently ignored. An advertisement's effectiveness might therefore be described by a bell-shaped curve, with one to three exposures as low, four to seven as high, and the curve thereafter tailing off again – a so-called 'normal' distribution curve.

In traditional media, advertising costs are not linked directly to effectiveness, but rather are most often determined solely by the number of impressions that a given publication or site can deliver in the target audience. These advertising rates are most usually quoted as a cost per thousand impressions, called a 'CPM'. CPMs for up-market business magazines are around $50 or more, for general magazines and newspapers around $10 to $20, and for TV around $5 to $15.

Measuring an advertisement's effect

An advertiser is therefore concerned with the potential audience a publication or poster site can deliver – in terms of its size and closeness of fit to the desired target market. CPM quotations allow a costing for the advertisement to be assessed. However, as well as these figures, it is also important to know the *'measurably quantifiable* subset', that is, it is important to be able to *count* the number of impressions with a knowable degree of certainty.

Magazine publications, for example, attempt to record the number of readers and to quote them in demographic and socio-economic groupings, that is, by factors like age, sex, employment status and income. In some cases – a subscription-only publication, for example – it is possible to know this audience with a high degree of precision; in others – such as low-cost, impulse-buy publications – it is far more difficult to be precise.

Influencing the audience

Finally, the advertisement exists to *influence* prospects. This might well require that the advertisement prompts an immediate purchasing decision; or it might require a more subtle influence, such as a steady but progressive change in consumer attitudes to a brand throughout the sequence of an advertising schedule. Alternatively, the influence might require second-order effects, such as where advertisers sponsor an event not because the event is necessarily attended by prospective customers, but because those customers will be pleased to purchase from a company responsible for such sponsoring.

Influence requires not only that prospects are *exposed* to the advertisement, but also that they are affected by it: that it gives them information on which they can act; or intrigues them into making an inquiry; or that it ensures the product name and brand identity is brought to mind. This has two aspects to it: firstly, the *positioning* of the advertisement; and secondly, the creative *content*.

In newspaper advertising, for example, the issue of positioning is particularly pertinent. While the publishers might have an excellent idea of the paper's readers, they cannot guarantee that a particular reader will in fact see each and every page. Most people read the newspaper in a specific pattern – scanning some pages briefly, reading others closely. The reading path through a paper involves the eye tracking a series of pages and positions within the page: some of these positions are more likely to be seen than others. Because of this, advertising rates in newspapers – and of course in other publications, such as magazines – are determined by where an advertisement is placed and hence its exposure.

Inside front covers, back cover positioning, even right- and left-hand page position all need to be considered. And this is not limited to print media: in TV commercial breaks it is important to position advertisements at an appropriate point. Viewers might be likely, for example, to leave the room during the break – a phenomenon well known to the electricity generating companies, who carefully monitor electricity supply as millions of kettles are set to boil during the breaks in the most popular shows. What this means, however, is that the mid-break advertising commercial position is less likely to be seen than the first and last slots, hence many advertisers try to buy *both* of these positions, using the last as a short 'reminder' of the core commercial message.

Finally, this issue of exposure tracking is also important in the layout of large shops and even the positioning of shops within centres such as airports. Shoppers rarely notice the items immediately inside a store, busy as they are adjusting to the change of pace involved in 'shopping' rather than in 'walking' (and this is often called the 'decompression zone'!). Advertisements and encouragement to explore goods therefore need to be carefully positioned with the key being an understanding of shoppers' habits and modes of thought.

The message itself is also, of course, important – and this is where the most apparent aspect of advertising skill appears: the *creative* ability. This is less about *imagination*, however, and more about *appropriateness*: advertisements should obviously ensure that the type and tone of message is appropriate for the audience – from sober presentation of information, to imaginative use of comedians, cartoons or highly active graphics. As we have said before, however, there is nothing new or magical in

Internet advertising as such: the purely creative element remains the same; what *is* different is the opportunity for presenting a more interactive message.

Advertising is clearly an art. Creating an imaginative series of images and messages is far from easy and calls for a specific set of skills. It is also, however, a *science* depending crucially on the ability to quantify the nature and size of a particular audience and the influence on them that it is possible for the advertisement to achieve. The points that are important in the context of the Web advertising hinge on this ability to reach a knowable audience and to be able to influence them in a trackable manner.

It is also worth noting in passing that the 'traditional advertising' world is dominated in a number of ways: firstly, it is an *immense* economy, with all the inertia and conservatism that that implies; secondly, there are a handful of very large corporations involved in the business of creating, placing and tracking the effectiveness of advertising in the 'traditional' media, supported by a range of specialist, *niche* businesses; thirdly, it has evolved a set of measuring concepts and established rules of thumb (four to seven impressions are effective; payment by CPM; effectiveness is assessed by impressions counted; no advertising on newspaper front pages; etc) that have worked well in existing media. Web advertising carries the potential fundamentally to alter many of these dominant ideas!

THE ELEMENTS OF WEB ADVERTISING

The basic building block of Web advertising is of course the sponsored Web page itself. In the Web, content really *is* king, and users have nearly complete control over their surfing progress. Some of these pages, however, are more attractive than others: they contain information that is of interest to a particular set of users – who might well be a target market for certain goods. Early Web advertising therefore involved simply using the graphics support provided by the Web to include a *logo* on the most popular pages, showing that the content was sponsored by the advertiser. As we mentioned in Chapter 1, this is in fact the *only* type of content-payment model widely available and used within the Internet: instead of *consumers* paying for the information, corporate *sponsors* pay for it.

Web users downloading the popular page would be presented with the sponsor's advertisement in a *passive* manner: the advertisement required no interaction or activity from the user. Early advertising models simply involved the advertiser paying the Web page owner – the *publisher* in effect – on the basis of the page's popularity; either a fixed monthly fee, or more usually a fee based on impressions similar to that involved in traditional media advertising. The 'legitimacy of presence' for the advertising message was assumed on the basis that viewers would appreciate that the popular page was in fact paid for and supported by the advertisers, just as the magazine or TV programme is supported.

In practice, of course, few readers or viewers consciously credit the sponsor with such support and so the legitimacy more probably arose as a result of *familiarity*: magazines and newspapers carry advertisements; the Web pages *looked* like magazine pages; therefore they could be expected to carry advertisements. For whatever reason, however, the excessive – but understandable – resistance to advertising in newsgroups was not experienced in the sponsored Web pages, encouraging the earliest Web advertisers to experiment further.

A particularly useful aspect of the Web is the ability to engage the user in a more active marketing message than can be achieved through the passive 'witnessing' of a magazine spread. The advertisers' objectives therefore gradually shifted from exposing the user to simple impressions, to enticing that user into visiting the corporate Web site of the advertiser – and there to be exposed to a more complete marketing dialogue.

As we have said, there are around 100,000 commercial Web sites, providing a range of on-line facilities. These are the 'shops', 'posters' and 'commercials' of the Internet and, as we shall see, can be established and operated easily and effectively although they can of course be very expensive to maintain. A commercial Web page, just like the amateur, 'hobbyist' pages, can contain graphics, sound clips, applets and so forth but, in this case, the elements are intended to serve a *commercial* purpose, rather than simply to demonstrate a level of technical competence.

A Web page is not like a fancy shop; 'build it well and they'll find *you*' is not appropriate to the Internet. The Web advertisers are therefore crucially dependent on the use of the links to their sites, which have evolved from the simple logos of early sponsoring into what are now called 'banners'. The most obvious application of advertising skill in the Web is now in the creation, placement and operation of these 'active advertisements'. This is also where the presence of publishers familiar to the advertisers become important: these links might typically be provided on the Web pages of on-line newspapers and magazines. Advertisers are therefore comforted by the ability to operate with essentially the 'usual suspects' even if in a wholly new environment.

The issues of creating and operating banner links; of establishing effective Web pages; of attracting and retaining an audience; and above all, of converting that audience into sales successes will all be considered in subsequent chapters. Before we begin to look at these issues, however, it is worth looking more closely at some of the opportunities and challenges posed by the process of Web-specific advertising: how can you tell your audience, and what can you do with them?

Demographics of the Web

Perhaps the most interesting aspect for the potential Web advertisers lies in the issue of demographics. Firstly, these are changing. A study by Nielson showed that in the period from August 1995 to April 1996, a broader range of users entered the Internet, primarily encouraged by the World Wide Web. These new users were less likely to be computer professionals, and to be from a much broader income, age and social mix: the Web is no longer the exclusive domain of the 'nerd'! Netscape, in fact, publish demographic data about the users of their browser software. This shows, for example, that around 50 per cent of their users are in the 26 to 45 age bracket; that 42 per cent have household income between $50,000 and $100,000 per annum, and that 77 per cent are in full-time employment. A well delineated and potentially attractive target market for many products.

A separate study in November 1996 showed that the male to female split of Internet users is now 68.6 per cent to 31.4 per cent, an improvement over the roughly 80–20 split of two years ago. This study also showed that the average age of Internet users has steadily risen to 34.9 years. Finally, although the figures *do* vary from study to study, it seems likely that the Internet population as a whole is currently between 50 and 100 million users, with some 35 million of these using the World Wide Web.

The second interesting aspect of these Web demographics, however, is *that they exist at all*!

As the previous section remarked, advertising serves a marketing programme, and these live or die on the basis of their understanding of the demographics and characteristics of target markets, audience and impressions. Web advertising is maturing and progressing. As we shall see, it is not yet perfect; however, a sufficient number of *other* advertisers have begun to use the facilities ensuring that a steadily more useful set of definitive measurements are emerging.

The opportunity is therefore relatively clear: a large, well-defined target market, with money to spend.

The global media myth

It is also, however, appropriate to register a few concerns about Web advertising as a whole. In many cases, the drive to advertise on the World Wide Web has come as much from imitation or perhaps a desire to innovate as it has from a real, hard-headed consideration of the cost-benefit ratios involved. Moreover, the field of Web advertising is subject to a number of pernicious myths: some of them inhibiting, but more of them introducing an unrealistic level of expectation. For example, a commonly quoted myth is that of global coverage.

It is certainly true that the number of Web users worldwide is counted in several tens of millions; and that the demographic mix is appropriate for certain products or services. However, it would be unwise to assume that this counts as a 'global audience' for *any* advertisement on the Web. Most obviously, the very nature of the Web means that the users must *choose* to download those Web pages containing explicit commercial messages. A Web site advertising certain goods will therefore only attract attention from a subset of the global audience, ie those who:

▶ know about its existence;

▶ are interested in the products and services; and

▶ *want* to receive the commercial message itself.

Some products and services are *definitely* of interest to almost all Internet and Web users. For example, by definition the Web users are potential customers for computer products. The Web population therefore has an almost perfect intersection with the target market for companies such as Microsoft and, of course, for the Web-specific vendors such as Netscape themselves. It should therefore come as no surprise to find that Microsoft, for example, topped the Jupiter Communications/AdLab tables of Web advertising spend in the fourth quarter of 1996, with almost $4 million – giving a cumulative year total of almost $10 million. (Interestingly, Netscape's spending in 1996 was around half of Microsoft's, but of course with Netscape's home page being one of the most popular sites, they have no need to spend on advertising fees on their own premises! In fact, Netscape's *income* from advertising topped that of Jupiter Communications, with well over $20 million for the year.)

For Microsoft and Netscape, however, the Web users are firmly and by definition a key (perhaps the *major*) part of their target market. For other advertisers, this is less clear. Ford, for example, were second to Microsoft in the AdLab table, with slightly more than $1.4 million in the third quarter, and $2.1 million in the fourth. The relationship between Ford's target market and the Web users is far from obvious, although it must be admitted that car manufacturers have been among the most avid of supporters for Web advertising: Ford, General Motors and Toyota all made the top ten of advertisers in that same spending table.

Why do they spend money on this advertising? Well, while the Web users do not represent more than a vanishing fraction of their target market, they *do* represent a specific audience – although whether the return on investment is appropriate is much less obvious. With an understanding of the audience characteristics, however, the car manufacturers can and do ensure that the commercial messages are appropriate.

For others, there has been a palpable belief that their products can receive *global* exposure through a corporate Web site. Had they spent the money on such global exposure through more traditional media, say TV advertising, it would have cost many, many times more than the expense of simply establishing a few Web pages. Well, this is true: it would certainly have cost more; and perhaps *because* it would have cost more, they would have considered the marketing programme more carefully, and then have decided that the likely return was not sufficient. These companies, from specialist manufacturers to global trading concerns, have all found that the Web is not the gold-mine they hoped it would be. In fact around 40 per cent of corporate Web sites were abandoned in both 1995 and 1996 as a result of this disappointing return. Hope springs eternal, however, and so yet more newcomers have arrived, confident that *they* will fare better.

As we have mentioned above, advertising exists to influence prospects into increasing the sales of products. It must therefore also be recognized that, while the Web is a global media of sorts, *spending* is more normally a local phenomenon: one might receive advertisements for products sold in other countries, but it is more likely that the products will be *bought* at a local shop. This is not to say that *purchasing* over the Internet does not occur: clearly it does, and it will be a growing element of world trade in the coming years. We will discuss it in more detail below. However, advertisers should consider the local as well as the global context of their advertisements. To borrow a quote from the conservationists: 'think globally, but act locally'.

The audience myth

The other aspect of the global media myth is not just that the audience is a global one, but also that it is a *passive* one – like the audience of a TV programme. The objective of a TV commercial is to keep a recumbent viewer passive through the commercial break. This is perhaps an oversimplification, but the essence is certainly true. Exciting and captivating images; interesting and amusing spokespeople; perhaps even intriguing and non-obvious images – these have all worked for TV advertisers ranging from car manufacturers, through banks to brewers.

Early Web advertisements mimicked this feature of the commercial break, assuming that a sufficiently captivating *image* would hold the viewer's attention long enough for the product *message* to be transmitted. Alas, the Web user is not recumbent; far from it. Surfing the Web is an *active* procedure, with users rapidly hopping from Web site to Web site. The issue for the advertiser therefore is not simply how to *captivate* the viewer, but also, how first to *attract*, then *retain* the viewer.

Web users must be enticed (some would argue, *lured*) to the Web site – and this is a problem we will address in the following chapter. However, once attracted, the Web advertiser has many advantages over the regular media advertiser: primarily, because they can choose whether or not to visit, we can assume that the viewer is *interested*!

An advertiser's dream...the targets of your on-line advertising are paying attention.[4]

MAKING THE LINK

As we discussed above, there are two ways in which the Web user can 'visit' a Web page: by typing the page's URL explicitly into the browser – which means they must of course *know* what it is; or by using a link from the current page, that in turn connects them to yours. In many cases, the link will be the usual route to your site but it is important not to overlook the obvious option of making sure that your prospects know your Web address directly.

There are several ways in which a Web user can be told about the link to your Web site. Most obviously, the site can be listed by one or all of the Web search engines. Many Web users consult these engines on a frequent basis, using them as their primary entry point into the broader Web. By indexing your Web site on the basis of your product, industry or business type and any other relevant key words, you can ensure that a user searching for a subject covered somehow on your Web site is provided with the necessary link.

In addition, the external marketing and advertising that forms a part of the broader programme or campaign can also reference your Web site: many newspaper, TV or magazine advertisements now include the URL for the advertiser's home page. Finally, business cards, letter-

---

[4] Levinson J C and Rubin C (1995), *Guerrilla Marketing on the Internet*, Piatkus, London.

heads, exhibition boards, product wrappers, etc can all carry the URL alongside your logo thereby ensuring that your existing customers or prospects are informed about the site.

Even if your marketing programme calls for all these elements, however, and the URL is known to as many Web users as possible, it is still not a guaranteed success. It is still necessary to *give the user a good reason to visit your site*. At the simplest level, this can be achieved by ensuring that they know what is on your site – through separate coverage in search engines, Internet-interest magazines, or through what is currently the most popular form of advertising link: the ubiquitous 'banner'.

BANNER ADVERTISING

4

A banner advertisement is a small, graphics link placed on a Web page. The banner is linked to the advertiser's Web pages, so that 'clicking' on it transports the browser into the advertiser's lair. Introduced first on the pages of a Web-published magazine – *HotWired*, companion to the traditional-media publication *Wired* – in October 1994, the banner advertisement has spread rapidly throughout the Web. Indeed, in the first three quarters of 1996, $156 million was spent on Web advertising, $138 million of it on banners; it is estimated that now around 11 per cent of Web sites carry advertising, the overwhelming majority of it in the form of a banner.

Advertisers believe that they understand them: after all, banner advertisements *look* deceptively like 'real-world' magazine advertisements; and because of this superficial similarity it seems also that Web users *accept* them as legitimate in context. Indeed, *Byte Magazine* in November 1996 found that only 31 per cent of readers surveyed found Web advertisements annoying; and a separate survey by *Advertising Age* found that over 10 per cent of users 'often looked' at advertisements, and that over 45 per cent 'sometimes looked'.

In many ways, banner advertisements are perhaps the 'purest' application of traditional advertising skills in the Web. Like real-world advertisements, they must provide a sufficiently persuasive enticement in a very small amount of space; unlike their paper-born cousins, however, banner advertisements have an effect that is directly and precisely measurable: users who click on the banner can be easily counted. What is more, the numbers can be recorded by the *advertiser* rather than by the publisher or a paid-for audit. So-called 'click-throughs' result in a browser user visiting the advertiser's Web pages and each such visit can be recorded.

CLICK-THROUGH RATES

The number of Web browsers who visit a Web page and subsequently click on the advertiser's banner is called the 'click-through rate'. When banners were first introduced, rates of 20 to 30 per cent were relatively common, in part because of the novelty of the concept. Over the last two years, however, the effectiveness of banners has decreased, and in general a very good click-through rate would now be around 3 to 8 per cent depending on how well targeted the banner was; for a handful of the most precisely targeted banners, click-through rates of 12 per cent are achievable; and one or two have achieved rates of 15 per cent, although this is now very, very rare.

This might be seen as a poor rate of return even for those advertisements that are precisely targeted in terms of the Web pages they occupy. For comparison, direct mail to homes might be considered as a substantially less well targeted form of advertising, yet in a 1996 survey in London, only 87 per cent of direct mail was found to have been trashed unopened; by analogy, this is a 'click-through rate' of 13 per cent (of course, mailers might then be trashed after having been opened – but a user clicking through to a disappointing site can equally well use the 'back' function on the browser!).

Having said that, however, banner success rates are *still* markedly better than response rates from regular print media campaigns, in which a figure of 0.15 per cent is not untypical. Is it fair to compare banner advertisements with direct mail or with newspaper response coupons? The answer can only be determined with respect to the type of broader marketing programme into which the Web-based advertising elements must be integrated – although intuitively for most cases one would expect the 'reply coupon' model to be the most satisfactory comparison.

To increase the effectiveness of what is an attractive form of on-line advertising for the traditional-trained advertiser, a number of studies have been undertaken to see how such banner advertisements might be developed. As well as the *technical* advances (that we will consider below), the *payment model* for the advertising banner has also progressed.

BANNER PAYMENT MODELS

The earliest of the advertising payment models was based on a simple, flat-rate fee with little or no association between the actual, or even the *expected* number of visitors to the site and the cost. Very quickly, however, this somewhat unrealistic state of affairs was replaced by payment models based more closely on the one-to-many broadcast model of traditional advertising and in particular, on the CPM model whereby advertisers pay on the basis of *impressions* of an advertisement. That is, advertising rates were calculated on the number of Web users accessing the Web page holding the banner.

In most cases, the *publishers* owning and operating the sites selling the advertising space will guarantee a number of impressions per month, and either price on the CPM basis, or provide a fixed monthly price with a quotation for the equivalent CPM. On the Netscape home pages, some of the most visited on the Web, for example, at the time of writing full advertising coverage promises around 2.25 million impressions per month, with CPMs around $20 to $25. The actual cost itself for total coverage on the Netscape Web pages is around $46,000 per month. On other Web sites, these CPMs can vary from as little as $10 to as much as $175; the mean is around $60, and the $10 rate is very rare.

By comparison to the more traditional media, this is a very expensive form of advertising – comparable to the ultra-well-focused advertising in profession-specific, subscription magazines. The other problem with this model is in the underlying principle itself. Magazine and other advertising is priced on the basis of impressions, purely and simply because this is the best that can be achieved in that medium. In the Web, however, impressions are not the 'best' for two reasons:

1. impressions are in fact difficult to assess precisely; and

2. a more precise measure than impressions is actually available – the 'click-throughs'.

Impressions are difficult to assess because site visits – the nearest the Web has to an 'impression' – are not what is recorded readily by the Web servers themselves. Recall from our discussion in Chapter 2, the Web servers receive requests to transfer page contents – that is, they receive 'hits' – and each page might require several hits to be satisfied, as different text or graphics elements are transferred. Which of these hits is to be recorded as the impression? Does an impression occur when the first part of the page is copied to the browser – or when it is *all* copied? What if the user chooses to interrupt a transfer, having already received part of the page – does this count as an impression or not? And if *unique* impressions are required – that is, a count of unduplicated visits – how is this to be achieved?

A calculation based on impressions alone is therefore fraught with difficulties and it would be unwise of an advertiser to rely on such a measure without an independent audit of the numbers involved. There *are* organisations that provide Web counter mechanisms that attempt to identify visitors uniquely, allowing the page to contain the now very popular 'odometer-style' counter, but even these are not a completely accurate measure. So-called 'cookies' can be used, with Web servers storing visitor information on the visitor's own browser so as to allow subsequent visits to be identified.

These and more sophisticated procedures are technically achievable, and the Web publishing industry is evolving ever more accurate counting mechanisms: there are around 40 separate organizations, for example, now dedicated to providing this advertising measurability within the Web. However, it is also worth considering an alternative to the impression – that is, the click-through itself.

Click-throughs

In April 1996, Procter & Gamble – among the earliest, most evangelical of the Web advertising enthusiasts – agreed with search-provider Yahoo! that they would pay advertising fees based not on CPMs but on click-throughs themselves. With a 1996 budget of $8 million for Web advertising, Procter & Gamble have a lot of influence – both with the content-providers such as Yahoo! and within the broader advertising community. The idea of paying for *results*, as it were, rather than *promises* is therefore gaining ever wider credence among the advertisers.

In the current model, the click-through payment is around the 25 cents mark. For the *publishers* this means that relatively high click-through rates must be supported. For example, to achieve advertising revenues equivalent to the $20 CPM currently enjoyed by Netscape, the click-through rate at 25 cents would have to be 8 per cent – high, but achievable with well-targeted banners. The norm click-through rate of 4 per cent would net publishers only $10 CPM equivalent, and to obtain the norm CPM of $60 would require a staggeringly high click-through rate of 24 per cent. Yahoo! itself quote CPMs of $100 for sponsoring a 'word' (discussed below); if Procter & Gamble only paid the 25 cent average for these click-throughs (unlikely), the rate would have to be 40 per cent!

For the *advertisers*, pay-by-click is advantageous: they are paying by results, after all. For the *publishers*, however, this is certainly not advantageous. In the current pricing model they are likely to receive lower advertising revenues for banner space; worse still, they are being rewarded or incentivized on Web-user activity over which *they have no control*.

A banner advertisement 'belongs' to the advertiser: they create it; they decide on its appearance and wording; they control its destination. If anyone can ensure the banner is effective, it is *them*. The owner of the Web page – the 'publisher' – has control of the pages on which the banner sits: they can make the pages attractive, interesting, relevant and appealing; they can guarantee that the host system on which the pages are held continues to operate 24 hours a day, seven days a week. If they control anything, they control the *audience*, but they cannot force that audience to attend the advertiser's site.

This is symptomatic of the fundamental shift of audience interactivity and choice that characterizes the move to the new medium – a shift that is unfortunately poorly appreciated by even the most ardent of Web supporters, and a shift that promises to alter our perceptions of mass-media communication dramatically over the coming few years.

For the advertiser to require payment by result is equitable, given *their* economic models; for the publisher to require payment by *impression* is also equitable, given the low degree of control they can possibly exercise over audience interactivity. Can the circle be squared? It can – by consideration of one further player: the advertising *agency* involved in the creation and placement of the advertisement.

The role of the agency

Advertising agencies in the traditional media world carry a varying load of responsibility for the advertising itself. Instructed on the overall marketing programme and product branding requirements, the agency – either directly or by subcontracting specialist firms – undertakes the creative work of 'inventing' an advertisement and persuading the advertiser – the product or brand owner, that is – that this is an appropriate style and message. They then – perhaps under guidance from the advertiser – arrange to buy media space, with placements on TV commercials, newspapers, posters, magazines and so forth.

The central advertising theme is therefore under the management of the advertising agency; the advertisement's success is up to them. Of course, as we said in Chapter 2, the Web is seen as a 'self-publishing' environment: it is easily possible for the advertisers to create and disseminate their own, DIY advertisements. For several reasons, however, this is a great mistake; we will consider why below. In most cases, therefore, the advertiser can be expected – and indeed, advised – to use an agency: either a specialist Web advertising agency (there are now many, very good ones) or the Internet-arm of one of the majors. (Indeed, a 1996 survey by Forrester Research found that nearly 60 per cent of major Web advertisers used the same agency for the Web *and* traditional media campaigns, thereby ensuring close integration of branding and message.)

An equitable model for both advertiser and publisher in banner advertising would then involve the 'payment-by-result' agreement with the advertising agency, in terms of an agreed click-through rate to the advertiser's site. For their part, the agency would then be faced with agreeing payment with the Web site publishers, based on the number of visitors received. Of course, this means that the counter mechanisms will have to be developed and refined, but this does have the advantage of being fair to all concerned.

Equitable payment models can therefore be established, even if it requires overturning what has become, even in just three short years, the 'accepted practice' of the industry. It is still essential, however, to make sure that the banner itself actually *works*, even within the limitations imposed by the mechanism itself. In this regard, two aspects of the banner are important: *where* it is placed; and *how* it looks.

THE SITE IS IMPORTANT

An obvious impact on the effectiveness of *any* advertisement – be it a Web banner or a roadside poster – is its location. On the Web, there are two aspects to this question: on which pages is the banner placed; and where on the page is it?

Choosing a page

The actual page on which the banner is placed is quite obviously going to be one of the major determining factors for how successful it is going to be. A well-focused Web page – that is, one that is attracting the audience appropriate for the advertisement – is clearly worth buying, even at very high advertising rates. Unless the prospects *see* the banner, they are certainly not going to click on it. Received wisdom, therefore, is that in the Web pages of the search engines, 'deeper' pages are worth more than 'higher' pages – that is, as the Web user specifies ever more precise search requirements, the Web pages reflect an ever more improved reflection of their interests and can therefore be expected to be more successful. Search engines therefore allow advertisers to sponsor particular search words, so that their banner is displayed on the pages appropriate to their product.

On this basis, as we have discussed above, Yahoo! CPMs are around $100 for banners attached to a word, and they in fact guarantee 10,000 impressions per month for that word. However, this focused interest might not necessarily turn into click-throughs – most obviously, because the search engine users are not searching for *advertisers* appropriate to a particular interest, but for Web *pages* appropriate to it. Simply attaching a banner, even to the most precisely focused search engine page, is not therefore any guarantee of click-through – perhaps exactly the reason why Procter & Gamble chose to renegotiate the basis of banner advertising fees with Yahoo! in the first place.

This is not to say that focused pages cannot make good banner sites; they can, of course, but the search engines themselves do not make the best vehicle for such pages. Far better are the Web pages of organizations or individuals that are directly relevant to the advertised product or service – such as *partner* pages. In this, two or more advertisers agree that any visitor to *their* site is also a potential visitor to another, hopefully non-competitive site. This form of 'cross-marketing' is familiar in the real world of retailing, where bundled offers are more commonplace. Within the Web, interest has begun increasingly to be shown in this field. Netscape, for example, have provided a range of cross-marketing agreements, with banner links supported to sites that agree to provide 'Netscape Now!' links back to them; others have done likewise. We will consider this development of the simple banner advertising principle in more detail below.

Banner positioning

As well as the Web sites and pages, the position of the banner on the page itself is also important. As Chapter 2 discussed, a Web page need not necessarily fit comfortably into a single screenful – and in fact in many cases pages run to several screenfuls. To read the whole page, users must therefore 'page down' through the text. Research undertaken early in 1996 found a marked difference of click-through rates for banners placed in the first screenful versus those in subsequent screens. Rates of 3.5 per cent to 4 per cent were observed for banners in the first screenfuls, but rates of only 0.5 per cent for those below the 'cut'.

This observation has interesting implications for the banner placement in many on-line publications, most particularly for newspapers. In traditional media, the majority of broadsheets carry almost *no* front-page advertising, and what they do carry is well away from the masthead itself. Many of the 'quality' broadsheets, for example, carry front-page adverts only at the very bottom right- or left-hand sides of the sheet – and certainly in the case of UK broadsheets, these advertisements are often for charities. Advertisements are then placed throughout the body of the newspaper with consideration to the reading habits of the average buyer.

The success rates for Web banners, however, implies that this placement is clearly not appropriate for on-line newspapers and in fact, that the banner advertisement should be granted equal prominence with the masthead itself. After all, the readers *know* the name of the newspaper already; attention to the sponsor's advertisement is perhaps the more important!

The ability to carry out dynamic and on-going assessments of a particular banner's success rate has also been used intelligently by advertisers – but most particularly by DoubleClick, who provide intelligent software agents to monitor banner performance. This agent can then be used to collect a constantly updated set of statistics, allowing the banner to be re-positioned and perhaps even re-deployed completely so as to increase the likelihood of that all-important click-through.

... AND SO IS THE SIGHT!

Once the banner has been placed on an appropriate page, in an appropriate position, the *appearance* of the banner itself then becomes the most important aspect. As Chapter Three observed, there is no 'royal road' to Web advertising success, and these banners should therefore be carefully designed. A significant advantage, however, is that although these banners are by no means guaranteed to succeed, they are sufficiently like the 'real-world' advertisements with which agencies –

and particularly, the *creatives* in those agencies – have had the most experience that designing their appearance is almost second nature.

First, there is the question of the wording of the advertising: the 'headline' and the 'copy'. The headline is the brief few words that introduce the advertisement; the copy is the more detailed text that supports and reinforces the message. In 'traditional' advertising it is frequently observed that a good headline almost always implies a successful advertisement; and that conversely, a poor headline can never be saved by even the most erudite of copy – the audience never bothers to read it!

In the banner context, the headline is usually the only text that is seen, with the subsequent copy on the target pages to which the banner links. Over the years, advertisers have found that there is a set of key words in the headlines that most often prove successful: 'you/yours', 'new', 'money/free', 'people', 'why/how' are all good words to use.

Second, there is the question of graphics, logos, cartoons and so forth: the actual colour and visual nature of the banner. Here, of course, the banner designer runs into the first of a series of problems associated with the Web medium itself. Primarily, loading graphics over the Internet can be a time-consuming and frustrating business: even when the image is a key part of the published Web page – rather than being an embedded advertisement – Web users are apt to lose patience and stop the transfer. Banners are therefore designed to be small, so that they are loaded as rapidly as possible. Netscape, for example, limit the size of these graphics files to just 10K. On the page, the banner graphic is therefore very small. Typically, the size is 468×60 pixels – less than 10 per cent of the screen itself.

There *are* many other sizes of banner graphics in common use ranging from 300 × 300 pixels for large 'box adverts' to 88 × 31 for 'micro buttons'. The size of the banner advertisement is clearly of interest both to the advertiser and to the Web page publisher: for the advertiser, it should be as large as possible, so as to have high visual impact; for the publisher, however, it should be as small as possible, so as not to distract from the page itself or delay the loading of the page. This balancing act seems to have resulted in the Netscape-style 468 × 60 banners being the most popular compromise.

There is a further issue with these banner sizes worth considering: the question of maintenance. If different Web publishers demand radically different sizes and even shapes of banners – or the smaller 'buttons' – then this leaves the advertiser having to maintain a series of different sized images. Submitting an inappropriately sized banner might well result in the image being drastically trimmed and thereby perhaps mutilated. In December 1996, several of the Web advertising organizations – under the Internet Advertising Bureau industry body – proposed a small set of standard banner sizes. In most cases, the now ubiquitous 468 × 60 banner will be the preference for advertising-supported sites, with a square button of 120 × 90 or 120 × 60 pixels or a micro-button of 88 × 31.

As well as the size of the graphic, advertisers should also consider the order in which the page is loaded by the browser. Initially, most pages load the textual content, followed then by the graphics. Because of this, it is important to provide the text of the banner headline as a hypertext link alongside the banner itself. In this way, the key headline message appears on the Web page almost immediately and will be sufficiently high up the page to be visible to the user while they wait patiently for the rest of the page – including the banner graphic – to be loaded.

As well as the question of a banner's size, graphics and textual content, there is also the issue of *exposure*. As Chapter Three discussed, traditional advertising 'rules' show that between four and seven impressions are required for a given advertisement to be recalled; and that there is an exposure count which advertisements should not exceed if they are to avoid becoming part of the background.

In Web advertising, this issue of effective- and over-exposure can be determined by analysis of the click-through rates, and an August 1996 study by DoubleClick showed that the first exposure resulted in click-throughs averaging 3.6 per cent; the next two exposures gained click-throughs at 2 per cent; thereafter, the click-through fell rapidly below 1 per cent. Unlike the 'Bell' curve of traditional advertising, it would seem that banner advertising sees an immediate and quite dramatic 'decay' – dubbed 'banner burnout'. Further research by I/PRO in late 1996, however, showed that this decay does not necessarily drop immediately to zero. In fact, their study[5] showed a click-through rate of 0.86 per cent even on the ninth exposure for many banners – and, as we have said, the 'reply coupon' response rate is typically around 0.15 per cent.

It is therefore far from the case that a banner is *useless* after three exposures, although its effectiveness *is* dramatically decreased. Clearly, however, the 'standard' rules of exposure do need rewriting in this context, since effectiveness *increases* with exposure for traditional advertisements up to a point, whereas banner advertising effectiveness begins to decay immediately. Because of this, successful advertisers change banners frequently.

---

[5] The study by I/PRO is reviewed along with others in the CyberAtlas site: 'www.cyberatlas.com'.

Netscape, for example, rotate banners on their pages at least every ten minutes, ensuring that visitors see as many different banners as possible and that, conversely, banners are not over-exposed. Clearly, however, the advertiser must ensure that new – perhaps themed – banners are continually provided to the publishers and that those publishers are willing to change the banners frequently.

A subsidiary point on exposure, however, is that the first three impressions – or at least, certainly the very first – must be used to the full. With less than 10 per cent of the screen allotted for the banner, it is all too easy for the Web user quickly to pass over the advertisement; that vital first impression is therefore lost. One facility that browsers and Web pages now support is the 'frame'. In this, the Web page is subdivided into regions – like windows – with scrolling available separately. Using these frames, advertisers can ensure that a frame is always available on the screen, holding the advertisement: the banner is therefore on show throughout the user's visit to the page.

A final point on general appearance: the Web supports a variety of mechanisms to allow banner graphics to be animated. Using 'animated graphics information format' (GIFs), a series of still images can be projected, giving a primitive form of animation. Simple cartoons, moving clockwork, jacks-in-the-box and so forth can all be supported in this very simple manner. In most cases it is possible to keep the banner graphics file below the preferred 10K size and yet still give these graphics options. Research undertaken in 1996 by a variety of advertisers showed that the effectiveness of a banner could be increased by a factor of 25 per cent by the simple step of including such moving images, even if just in a limited series of linked, still images: a developing and evolving 'story' is often enough to capture attention – and if the banner poses a question to the user, exciting their curiosity, its effectiveness can be improved still further.

An alternative to animated graphics is also available, provided by the now increasingly widespread Java applets. These are tiny programs that are downloaded in place of the graphics and are executed within the browser. Instead of a simple series of still images, these can be far more sophisticated. We will consider these in more detail in the following chapter.

As well as the general appearance and position of the banner on the page, it is also necessary to encourage the viewer to *use* the banner. One very simple addition to even the most colourful, active and imaginative of banners has been found to increase their effectiveness fourfold: the words 'Click here'! Again, this might seem patently obvious, but has been overlooked in all too many cases.

Finally, the user has to be given some simple encouragement or enticement to visit the site itself. Within the limited banner space it is seldom possible to create the most enthralling of dialogues – and so it has been argued by many that banners are clicked on only if the user is already aware of and interested in the advertiser's site. This, however, need not be so: it *is* possible to encourage 'strangers' to the site through a banner. In some cases, banner advertisers have found it necessary to try offering inducements such as free gifts, but surveys of Web users show that they are more interested in *information* than *freebies*.

Some simple and effective banner advertising strategies are therefore to use a known, 'talking head' on the banner, offering the answer to an intriguing question on the advertiser's Web pages. For example, an electricity company might try a banner style with a phrase like: 'Do *you* know how the electricity reaches your home? Click to find out'. Car manufacturers might offer a tour of their production plant; chocolate manufacturers might offer a guide to where and how the ingredients are made, etc.

Although the demographics of Web users *are* changing, most are still in the top educational, social and employment brackets – they do not *need* free gifts, but they might have an *interest* in learning something new.

A last thought on the use of simple banner advertisements: it might *never* be clicked on by the user! This is an unfortunate but realistic observation; experience shows, as discussed above, that click-through rates of more than 5 per cent are a rarity for your banner. Now, it is of course possible to respond to this by making the most enticing, alluring and provocative banner imaginable – and lots of advertising creatives take this approach. However, even if the click-through rate can be raised to the dizzy heights of 20 per cent (and it *can*!), that still leaves 80 per cent who will only see the banner itself – in effect the junk mail envelope or the simplest headline of a magazine spread.

A sensible response to this problem is therefore to ensure that *some* simple message about the product or advertiser is available, even if just their name! This might sound a trivial point, but many of the banner advertisements overlook the simple notion of making sure that a passing Web user sees their name or logo, is perhaps reminded of their catchphrase and thereby allows the banner to serve what is admittedly a minimal purpose, but a purpose nonetheless.

SUMMARY

Although banners have very many problems associated with them, they are by far the most popular form of advertising within the Web at present. To use a banner advertising strategy successfully, it is necessary to consider many aspects, summarized below:

1. Ensure that the banner advertisement is presented in a prominent area of an appropriately interesting Web page. Recall, click-throughs are very low in general, but can be optimized by the use of well-targeted advertisements that appear on the first screenful of the Web page.

2. Refresh the banner very often. Click-throughs decay once the banner has been seen more than once. Themed or linked banners can be used to maintain a common, developing storyline to the banners, but it is important to make sure that Web users see a different image at different times.

3. Use action words ('click here') and the headline key words that have been proved effective in other contexts; use 'talking heads' and encouragement through the offer of *information* – albeit presented in an imaginative and entertaining way – rather than possibly inappropriate free gifts.

4. Keep the size of the banner to the standards acceptable to the publishers – for preference, 468 × 60 pixels and limited to 10K. If possible, require the Web publisher to place the banner in a frame so that it remains permanently visible – and if appropriate, use animation so as to draw the user's attention to the message.

And always remember, there is no royal road on offer in the Internet and it is the *users'* choice whether or not to click-through to your site. Your banner is the small encouragement – the enticement, or the *bait* – but it might also be the only part of your site or Web presence that they see. It is important, therefore, that your banner also makes sure that even the passing visitor *knows* who you are! A banner that is intriguing, imaginative but does not give your company name, or perhaps your trademark, logo or an associated 'catch phrase' is a *wasted opportunity*.

BEYOND THE BANNER 5

Banner advertising has achieved a wide range of things in the field of on-line marketing. By being apparently familiar in structure, the banner tempted many advertisers to try their luck in a novel medium; and by being sufficiently *different*, the banner has forced those advertisers gradually to rethink and to develop their mastery of that medium. More than this, the familiarity of the banner to the *user* has allowed that 'legitimacy of presence' for on-line advertising to be established; so that now, 'Netiquette' notwithstanding, advertising and commercial practices are a growing element of the Internet world: the Cybernation's marketplace is steadily evolving.

However, despite the still growing numbers of banner advertisers and advertisements, voices – particular among the professional advertisers – have begun to be raised against the banner: the low click-through rates, high cost and size limitations make it far from ideal. What is more, while the banner has gained some acceptance for on-line advertising, there are still those Web users who despise advertising of any form, and who have developed and distributed sophisticated filtering tools to excise the simple banner and logo from Web pages directly! As we commented in the previous chapter, the Web is the ultimate interactive medium, in which a user has near-total control over where they go and what they see.

As on-line advertising expertise has developed, many have therefore made the case for going 'beyond the banner': for providing new advertising schemas and approaches, that more obviously benefit from the inter-activity and inter-linked aspect of the medium itself; or that intelligently exploit the technical facilities on offer.

This is still early days, and the novel approaches have only recently begun to be explored but already there are a number of attractive alternatives. The banner itself can be expanded and developed using the new technology of executable content, or by taking advantage of browser-held information; or the distribution and arrangement of advertising sites can be improved; or more sophisticated advertising mechanisms can be employed; or the newest of the Web 'push' technologies can be used to provide targeted, commercial break-style messages.

In this chapter we will introduce the more interesting of the novel approaches that have been seen or that are simple, logical developments from the present schemes; however, it should be recognized that such developments are coming ever faster. This is likely to be far from the last word on the subject!

EXTENDING THE BANNER

Perhaps the first and most obvious steps that can and have been taken to extend banner advertising in general lie in the area of straightforward extensions to the basic banner mechanism itself. The research described in the previous chapter shows that banners are dissimilar in their actions from the 'standard' advertising format – not surprising since they are received and considered in the intelligent and interactive environment of a user's network-connected PC. One of the simplest approaches to extending the simple banner is therefore to accept this difference and to use the 'programmability' of the computer on which the advertisement is displayed, so as to create new and interesting shapes, images or messages whenever the banner is seen. A simple means of doing this is, for example, by using the facilities of Sun's 'Java' or Microsoft's 'ActiveX' applets.

Using Web applets

An 'applet' is a small program or set of instructions copied from a Web server on to the local browser, just like the graphics and textual content of old. With these applets, however, instead of merely fulfilling a simple display role, the browser can execute the program locally. The nature of the Java language, for instance, allows for several concurrent parts of the program to be executed simultaneously; each part is called a 'thread' and can be used to gather information, animate pictures, or to perform the most complicated of software functions. Both Java and ActiveX are complete program languages, able to do almost any permitted software task.

For example, Java-animated snowflakes have been produced by one advertiser, with each snowflake generated individually, so as to produce a unique pattern each and every time. This image has been used to support the concept that, in this case, each pair of a particular brand of jeans is unique, just like the snowflake image. Similarly complicated images – spinning DNA, building bricks, etc – have been used by others.

Web applets have also been used within banners to provide simple yet engaging computer games such as the basic ping-pong games familiar from the very earliest of home computer systems. For many of these 'banner-games', the success has been quite dramatic, recalling the earliest days of the simple banner advertisements. Others have gone beyond *games*, to offer more useful programs: for example, a food magazine's banner advertising featured an embedded applet and reply-form to allow users to search an on-line database of recipes. The click-through rate for this banner reached over 50 per cent!

Such enhanced banners – that provide a usable and useful function within themselves – are becoming ever more popular, primarily because of this high success rate. A so-called 'Virtual Tag' banner mechanism has been produced by First Virtual, allowing information and on-line ordering to be completed within the banner. As well as ordering, the use of Java applets in the 'live' banner allows the images to move and evolve as the mouse is moved around the screen: instead of a simple, sequential series of images in an animated GIF, the banner can develop and progress in a captivating manner.

At the moment, these new types of Java-enabled banner are popular both with the advertisers *and* with the Web users: click-throughs of well over 20 per cent are far from uncommon. Whether this is similar to the initial popularity of the basic banner and can be expected to tail off throughout this year only time will show. The important point, however, is that the basic banner mechanisms have been developed in new, imaginative and creative ways – and this development is taking into account the interests and habits of the Web users themselves.

There are other elements of modern browser technology that can equally well be applied by the on-line advertisers to capture attention. For example, the on-line magazine *Word* [6] – developer of the initial set of Microsite

---

[6] See 'http://www.word.com' for these Microsite and subliminal pages.

pages – at the time of writing carry so-called 'subliminal' advertisements. In this case, an intermediate page is introduced between two content-full pages. This page contains a banner link, or even a larger graphics adver-tisement. The clever trick, however, is that the page automatically jumps to the next content-full page after only a few seconds. Few can resist going back to the page and trying to 'catch' the link before it vanishes!

In time, of course, this trick also will become overused, and advertisers will move on to new mechanisms. After applets, perhaps the next most obvious prospect is that of browser 'cookies'.

Using cookies

In Chapter 2, we described the organization of the In-ternet. Recall, connections between server and client systems are a short-lived affair only long enough for a simple request to be issued and satisfied; thereafter, the server in effect 'forgets' about the client until the next request. This – as we discussed – leads to difficulties in *counting* Web accesses on an individual page; it also means, however, that the servers have little or no sense of 'state' or of 'context' in their communications.

This can be seen as a difficulty in several practical situ-ations: consider an on-line shopper. When the shopper chooses goods – by whatever mechanisms – it is neces-sary to maintain a record of these choices. Holding this record on the server is problematic: subsequent infor-mation requests from the client are difficult to associate with earlier ones, so as to build a consistent record of purchasing sessions; also, for how long must the infor-mation be retained? Instead, the data can be stored on the *browser* or client end, available to the server for update as subsequent selections are made. When the shopping session is complete, the server needs simply to examine the collected records and use this to place the order and invoice.

The data stored on the local browser is referred to as a 'cookie': crumbs left behind as a trail of browser activity. These cookie files are accessed by the Web servers and read or set as appropriate: they allow a form of 'transaction state' to be introduced into the *stateless* Web protocols.

From an advertising perspective, they are very useful. Browser-held information in general can provide the servers with a wide range of information about the browser user: their geographical location and browser type in particular. The true power of cookies for advertising comes, however, from the *setting* of values that indicate which of a series of advertisements have been seen by a particular browser. As we have already seen, the effectiveness of a specific banner declines dramatically after the first exposure, dropping close to zero after a mere half dozen or so views. By recording which banners have already been seen, a Web publisher can ensure that only the unseen banners are displayed.

Cookies can also be used in more sophisticated ways. In particular, the cookie can be used to record the *location* of the browser, so that only advertisements for a specific country or even city are displayed; recall from above, 'think global, act local'. Alternatively, cookies can be used to track the path through a series of Web pages or shopping choices (called a 'click trail'); or even criteria for searches performed by search engines. This information can then be used to construct a *profile* of the user so that only those advertisements for a particular Web page or site that are relevant to them are in fact displayed.

For example, if a given search engine user can be seen to search regularly for material on various racquet sports, sportswear manufacturers and for reports of current tennis matches, it might well be advantageous to display advertisements for upcoming, local tournaments or the like. Notice, this is different from linking banner advertisements to particular search *terms*; instead, the profile or search usage is built up over a long period of time and is specific to the user's interests as exposed by analysis rather than by immediate and simplistic observation. So-called 'agents' able to perform this analysis – such as 'Firefly' – have become ever more widespread as advertisers try to extract the most detailed and usable information from the habitual patterns of visitors. Based on this analysis, only the most appropriate and potentially interesting banners would be presented and thereby, they hope, be all the more successful.

More risky, it has been suggested that the complete set of cookies held on a given user's browser – including records of books bought, shops and sites visited, search terms regularly used, etc – could all be used to create a very comprehensive profile, more comprehensive even than that obtained by asking the user to complete a questionnaire form. In the computer security world, programs able to collect these several disjoint sets of cookies are familiarly called 'cookie monsters'. Such an analysis would of course be far more detailed than that available to an individual Web site cookie analysis, which would normally only retrieve those values that it had previously set in earlier 'sessions'. There is, however, the obvious fear of privacy invasion through this sort of analysis – with hackers or others able to examine a browser user's activity on unrelated Web sites throughout the Internet – although whether it falls foul of the various European Union countries' data protection laws remains to be seen.[7]

One way around this problem would be for the *user* themselves to create and define their own profile of

interests – by completing a particularly detailed questionnaire – and to offer this for use by the advertisers as
an effective filtering mechanism, thereby reducing the
advertisers' costs. In many ways, this would dramatically
shift the emphasis on advertising choice from the *advertisers* to the *shoppers*. Indeed, commentators on the future vision of electronic commerce and on-line living
have seemed to split along a fault-line between these
two views.

Those with a strong marketing background – such as Bill
Gates of Microsoft – write of the power of on-line advertising to focus only appropriate advertisements on a
given consumer, thereby ensuring advantages to the
advertiser of little or no wasted effort. By contrast, Nick
Negroponte, Ray Hammond and others write of the
power of *choice* and selectivity offered to the *consumer* in
downloading and acting on only those advertisements
appropriate to them.[8]

Cookie Monster or weaker analysis of Web server-col-
lected personal profiles would support the marketers'
vision of focused advertisements; personally-developed
and offered profiles – perhaps using identical mechanisms in practice – would of course satisfy the libertarian
vision. Given that the broad pattern of development in
the Web has seemed to concentrate on enabling the
individual, one would have to presume that this would

---

[7] The information is stored and processed by the *user* on their own systems, albeit
under the direction of the Web server software. In this case, there is no sense in
which a data set is collected and analysed by an organization needing to register
its use under the Data Protection Act. This is a 'grey' area, requiring careful
thought. In the US, there are no equivalent data protection laws, although there
is a much stronger sense of personal privacy protection of which such activity
would fall foul.

[8] See Gates, B (1996) *The Road Ahead*, Viking, New York; Negroponte, N (1995)
Being Digital, Hodder & Stoughton, Sevenoaks; Hammond, R (1996) *Digital
Business*, Hodder & Stoughton, Sevenoaks.

be so in this case also, and that the libertarian view would tend to dominate in the coming years – an important observation for the challenges that advertising and on-line commerce must face if it is to be successful.

Whether through the introduction of sophisticated applets or by the use of intelligent cookie analysis – or simply through the imaginative use of moving images, humour and simple creativity – the banner mechanism is sure to develop further. While it *is* certainly the case that the banner is far from perfect – as many advertisers freely admit – there is unlikely to be a rapid move away from them, particularly because advertisers, publishers *and* (most of the) audience accept and understand them.

As well as developments in the *nature* of the banners, however, there have also been parallel developments in the *publishing* models for those banners. Taking advantage of the 'self-publishing' nature of the Web medium, several advertisers have moved towards a 'banner exchange' mechanism rather than a formal sponsoring arrangement.

Banner exchange mechanisms

In most cases of traditional media and even on-line advertising, the process of the advertising sponsorship itself has followed a well-established model: advertisers have sought out an agency, tasking them with the process of devising and placing an advertising schedule within a series of appropriate publications. An important aspect of the advertising agencies' job, therefore, has been the purchasing of this 'space' from the journals, newspapers, TV broadcasters or whatever – acting as an intermediary for the advertiser in question.

In the world of the Internet, however, it is easily possible to 'cut out the middleman' – a process formally referred to as 'disintermediation'.[9] In this, two Web advertisers agree to carry each other's banner advertisements on one another's Web sites – assuming that each site is well visited. By cross-linking the sites in this way, a wider audience can be guaranteed. Of course, there are two problems that must be addressed: first, the two advertisers must ensure that each is getting appropriate coverage, ie that the banners are equivalently positioned, and that the sites see roughly equivalent levels of traffic. They must also, of course, ensure that they are not *direct* competitors!

Second, however, they must *contact* one another. Throughout the Web a number of banner and link exchange schemes have emerged, with interested parties able to provide a central database with information about their sites, traffic and interest areas. Through this exchange – almost a 'dating agency' for Web advertisers – they can arrange sharing details with one another. In many cases, the exchange itself provides a free service: this is *true* disintermediation; in others, the exchange might seek a profit through a charging mechanism. In either case, however, the process of agreeing to share banners is an arrangement for the advertisers themselves.

This form of 'do-it-yourself' is increasingly popular in the Web and, indeed, leads to difficulties in assessing the actual levels of banner and other advertising forms in use. It is only really possible to measure the *spend* on advertising through agencies or others that publish or record the details. If ever more is performed on an essentially amateur basis, measuring becomes more difficult; and if there is in fact *no* payment for the banners, it becomes *impossible* to measure.

---

[9] For a more detailed discussion of the role of disintermediation in the emerging on-line economy, see Tapscott, D (1996) *The Digital Economy*, McGraw-Hill, New York.

A problem with the DIY approach, however, is that very amateurism. Banner exchange contracts might not in fact be equitable; and the banners themselves might be clumsy and poorly executed. One party to the exchange might have a low grade site – notwithstanding anything they might have said to the 'dating agency' – or might attract a wholly unsuitable audience. Indeed, a major problem in Web page sponsoring is this issue of first locating and then continuing to monitor those sites on which an advertiser would like to place a banner. While banner exchanges *have* grown in popularity, they are therefore not widely used by the *big* advertisers, although Netscape, for example, do indeed carry out a form of banner exchange, providing reciprocal references for many of the sites that carry the ubiquitous 'Netscape Now' button.

The technical and commercial elements of advertising banners are therefore sure to continue to develop, at least for the next few years. Banners, however, are just one simple mechanism whereby commercial advertisers can associate their products, services or good name with a Web page. There are many others, developed from the tried and tested approaches first developed in the early years of publishing and broadcast media. The most obvious such is that of direct, formal *sponsoring* of that content.

SPONSORING CONTENT

The banner emerged as a simple mechanism for explicitly transporting a Web user from a sponsored page to those pages belonging to the sponsor themselves: an obvious doorway linking the two sites, and that was knowingly used by the Web browser. However, as reluctance to use those links has gradually increased – even if the links themselves have been granted a degree of legitimacy of presence – and even as the banner technology itself has progressed, advertisers have begun to question the fundamental assumptions inherent within the very banner advertising model itself.

First, as we observed above, the banner gained acceptance with publishers, advertisers and users simply because it appeared familiar in form even if it was unfamiliar in operation. The realization that has gradually developed over the last year or so, however, is that such a familiar mechanism might not in fact be ideal within an interactive, interlinked environment: for 'familiar', perhaps now read 'old-fashioned' or even 'unimaginative'. An expectation that the visual structure in particular associated with cheap advertisements successful within magazines and newspapers would be equally successful in a dynamic, user-driven new medium is now, in retrospect, seen as naive.

Second – and perhaps even more tellingly – there is an obvious question that is now being asked: Why link the user to the sponsor's site *at all*? What is important is that the prospective consumer views not the sponsor's *site*, but rather the *content*. And if the user must be enticed to the sponsor's content, why must that necessarily imply that the content is held on the sponsor's *own* site – and if it *must*, why must the link be an explicit one?

Web advertisers are presented with many, *many* more opportunities to deliver their content to the Web user than are available through the operation of a simple – and essentially *simplistic* – banner link. Content is king, an observation that underpins all analysis of the operation of the Web: users 'surf' not for entertainment, not blindly following the next most interesting link, and not in a haphazard way. They surf for *information*: to answer a question, to satisfy a requirement; to *find* something. That something might well be entertaining but the actual act of surfing itself is not; and of course, with many Web users accessing the facilities from home, over a telephone line, at least outside the US there is an ever present concern over the cost of the telephone call itself.

Banners do not work – or rather, do not work as well as was hoped – simply because they are not a part of the Web surfers' 'search pattern'. This observation was presented in the context of search engines themselves but it is also appropriate in a much wider set of contexts throughout the Web structure. The clear message from this analysis therefore is this: successful Web advertisers must ensure that their content – their commercial messages and enticements – are included as part of the users' search and surf patterns, rather than as a separate, free-standing and easily ignored part.

Product placement

Perhaps the simplest and most obvious model for this is that of 'product placement'. A sponsor's product – a soft drink, a motor vehicle, clothes, etc – is used and presented in a blatant and explicit manner within the film, TV show or even novel. Initially clumsy, the sophistication of this sponsorship model has progressed dramatically in traditional media – particularly film – so that it is now a widely accepted and widely used element of commercial support.

The application of this approach to the Web pages is reasonably easy to see. At the simplest level, the sponsor's messages could be weaved throughout the content of a sponsored Web page: where reference to a generic item is required, the sponsor's specific product could be mentioned. This is sometimes called 'content co-branding'. An example might be a sponsorship deal between a jeans manufacturer and the operators of a Web site covering American cowboy history.[10] Jeans are associated with cowboys, and so it might well be appropriate for the manufacturer to have a presence on that site. Throughout the site, their particular products can be mentioned, with graphics clearly illustrating the brand as necessary.

This is certainly preferable to the alternative approach of a simple banner link. After all, a visitor to a cowboy history site is interested in potentially a wide variety of subjects: cowboys themselves, the 'wild west', perhaps even the Indian wars, cattle driving, the development of handguns, etc. *Some* might be interested in denim trousers, but they can be expected to be a vanishingly small percentage. Where banner advertising has fallen down, however, is in the observation that *all* of the visitors to the site can be expected to be jeans wearers, and that the commercial message is therefore not only legitimate in context (after all, there *is* an obvious association between cowboys and jeans) but also appropriate to the audience.

To reiterate, Web surfers are in the main *looking* for *information*. A banner link to a jeans manufacturer's site will therefore only really attract those whose interest is in whatsoever a jeans manufacturer might have to say. This is perhaps the primary reason why banner advertising is accused sometimes of having failed to deliver adequate returns.

Weaving a commercial sponsorship thread throughout the text and content of a Web page is therefore preferable. After all, it is then possible to present the content in such a way that the Web user sees it in context, does

---

[10] I'm not aware of such a sponsorship deal in practice: this is intended as a simple illustration, although I am sure that there are a large number of equivalent examples available 'in the wild'.

not have to choose to hunt it out, and is exposed to a more subtle and above all suitable message. There is, however, a problem with such blatant product placement: they all too easily become 'advertorial' sites and are then criticised for compromising the site content itself. This, of course, is a problem equally associated with unsubtle product placement in films or TV shows: all too often, such product placement inevitably reduces the very interest on which it is dependent.

Where a sponsor has paid substantial sums of money – and in the case of many sponsored Web sites, figures of $20,000 to $50,000 per month have been reported; high, compared to the cost of banners – there is a significant temptation to tailor the site explicitly to (over) emphasize the placed product or message, and thereby gradually erode the value of the site itself. In the case of the jeans example, most obviously the particular brand might not have been developed at the time of the cowboys!

A better solution to such 'content weave' problems could be presented by the use of so-called 'Microsites'.

Microsite sponsorship

In the case of banners, the link is expected not only to take the Web user to the sponsor's site, but also to their *generic* content. As we will discuss in Chapter 6, most Web publishers and advertisers at least initially developed Web sites that were little more than electronic versions of traditionally published information sources: an on-line newspaper or magazine, or an electronic version of the corporate brochure. Through 1996, many of these sites developed in sophistication and imagination – but it was still the case that the Web site was *the* Web site, and that the very many banner links spread on pages throughout the World Wide Web were intended to bring visitors into the main entrance to the corporate Web site.

In the case of our example of a jeans manufacturer, this might well mean that users enticed from a page on cowboy history arrive at a corporate Web site dedicated to celebrating the role of denim in a youth culture. There is of course little or nothing to retain the interest of such viewers – even though some of the commercial messages might on deeper inspection be found to have some relevance. Alternatively, the more sophisticated banner users began to make the links to more directly relevant elements of their main site, although the messages were still of course essentially generic in nature.

By contrast to this generic aspect, the idea behind the use of Microsites is that the sponsor funds or provides a small set of pages – much smaller than the primary corporate ones – that are immediately and specifically of interest to the visitor to the sponsored site. Usually these have been associated with so-called 'infotainment' sites: Web-published magazines, for example, where the Microsite acts almost like a newspaper insert. These Microsites have sometimes also been called 'brand modules' or even 'cuckoos', since they are 'eggs' placed in another bird's nest! In some cases, the Microsites are very small indeed: sometimes just a single page, providing a so-called 'bridge page' from the sponsored content to the sponsor's Web site.

The important point is that in the Microsite or brand module idea, the pages are developed specifically – perhaps in conjunction with the publisher of the sponsored site – to follow *their* basic structure, presentational feel, and to be intimately embedded with the core content, without compromising it.

In the case of the cowboy site, for example, an appropriate part of the main page set might include a reference to the importance of hardwearing clothes, with a link to a set of pages providing a history of cowboy fashions, gradually introducing the role of denim and hence of the brand itself. In this way, the sponsor's content is introduced in an appropriate and acceptable way. The Microsite can make it clear that the set of pages is sponsored – or can choose to disguise the fact; it can even include an explicit link to the sponsor's site for those interested in more information about the particular brand.

A point to consider in this case is that such a link need not follow the internal rules of *banners* but rather of more general, informational links: the link need not appear in the first screenful, be updated frequently, or work overhard at attracting attention. Moreover, those users that *do* follow the link represent a substantially more interested audience for the sponsor's content than those enticed or even 'fooled' into visiting. In this way, the sponsor is working *with* the Web philosophy of content rather than in spite of it.

These Microsites have been used by a variety of successful advertisers: VISA, for example, sponsored such a collection of pages within Yahoo!, and the Web publishers GNN have invited a whole series of advertisers to provide such sponsored page collections within relevant parts of their on-line magazine publications. In many ways Microsites – particularly the smallest bridge pages – provide a convenient halfway house between full Web sites and the more limited banners. Banners and bridge pages, however, can be seen to be rapidly converging, particularly where the bridge has been provided within a frame on a sponsored-content page. As with the Java-enabled banners, this is a fast progressing aspect of Web advertising.

The sponsorship process

While the Microsite or more intimate sponsorship is more likely to be successful than the simple banner links, there is still the question of ensuring that the sponsorship deal itself is successful. Because of the essentially amateur nature of the World Wide Web, the earliest of these sponsorship deals were little more than reciprocal agreements to provide cross-links between appropriate sites. There was little or nothing in the way of formal commercial pacts. The hypertext nature of the Web means that these associations are easy to establish in practice and so there was a reasonable but erroneous assumption that the legal elements should be equally simple to establish.

In making a formal sponsorship arrangement, the sponsor must ensure that a wide variety of contractual conditions are put in place: where will the links to their sponsored content appear; what guarantees does the Web site owner provide against system failures, or even damage from the activity of hackers; does the owner agree not to carry rival products, or elsewhere to undermine the credibility of the sponsor's brand in this context; who has responsibility for maintaining and updating the Microsite pages? These are just the most obvious, practical considerations that must be addressed, and must be agreed in the context of a formal, written contract. While the Web *is* a hobbyist environment, for *commercial* users it should be seen as entirely within their more established, traditional-media practices.

It is also necessary to establish the conditions under which the sponsored site will gain any additional revenue. In particular, it might be the case that as a result of a link from a sponsored site, products are sold. This is a growing element of the Web as full electronic commerce solutions are beginning to become available. In this situation, it would be entirely appropriate to reward the sponsored site for its effectiveness.

As an example, Amazon has begun to offer a commission to those sites providing links to its on-line bookstore where those links result in a sale. A normal commission payment for such sales might be between 2 and 3 per cent; by contrast, Amazon offer 8 per cent. Sites that mention a particular book can therefore link to the Amazon site pages selling that book, providing users with a secure, workable and above all trustworthy way of obtaining the book on-line. At the end of 1996, some 3500 referencing sites had joined the Amazon scheme, which seems set fair to provide a model used more widely within the Web.

Sponsored sites and Microsites therefore provide a good alternative to the less imaginative use of simple banner links. Both technically and contractually they must be well built and appropriate, and it is important always to consider their content. If they have a problem, it is that the content *must* be so very well tuned – leading of course to increased maintenance costs. It is true that such maintenance – and even the development itself – can be provided by the sponsored-site owner, but this weakens the sponsor's control of the material. Top-end sponsorship deals of $50,000 per month are therefore expensive, particularly so because this is just the merest fraction of the broader costs likely to be uncovered.

Because of these practical considerations, advertisers are also looking at alternatives to the interactive medium of banners and Web sites altogether. In particular, to what is widely perceived as a return to the traditional 'push' form of broadcast advertising within the Web.

SCREENSAVERS AND PUSH BROADCASTING

In part, the initial clumsy attempts at on-line advertising can be seen as having been approaches to duplicating the traditional-media models within a wholly new, interactive medium with which the advertisers, publishers and even users had little or no practical experience. Complex Web sites, banner links and so forth are all obviously descendants from the more easily understood marketplace of magazines, TV shows and commercial breaks – with Web advertisers slowly and painfully learning those things that make on-line advertising different in nature, and therefore the requirements for changes in those advertising mechanisms transferred from the print or broadcast media.

In parallel with the banner links and sponsored sites, recent technical and creative developments have in fact also allowed Web advertisers to return, as it were, to their roots more directly. In particular, two specific elements have allowed advertisers to 'resurrect' the commercial break within the new media context: on the one hand, the widespread use of so-called screensavers; and on the other, the very recent emergence of 'push' Web broadcast models.

Screensavers

By far the most popular of computing devices – in the home and in the office – is the near universal PC, most usually running one or other of the Microsoft Windows operating systems. A feature of these, obvious to any user, is that an idle monitor almost inevitably begins to display a screensaver image. There are a wide variety of these: simulations of stars flowing past a speeding spaceship; bouncing balls, oscillating lines, rapidly spinning shapes – even flying toasters.

In 1995, Guinness released a new screensaver on to their Web pages, freely available for users throughout the world to download. It was not the first such commercial screensaver (there had been earlier, clumsy attempts at simple messages) but it did become the most widespread. This screensaver displayed a long sequence of images from the then current advertising campaign, along with the advertisement's music. When the screensaver began to work, it was exactly as though the PC monitor had begun to show a true, TV-style commercial break. Elsewhere, I have written of these as 'smartverts': smart advertisements that are pulled on to or that invade a user's PC. I predicted that they would grow in popularity[11] and, at the time of writing, they have done just that, with very many advertisers making available a host of copycat schemes.

The Guinness and other screensavers are a godsend for the advertisers. They provide yet another medium in which the visual and audio aspect of ongoing commercial break advertisements can be displayed. They capture passing attention – provided that they are interesting and entertaining enough to be installed in the first place. Most important, however, for the advertisers is that they need not be supported by a wholly new, interactive-media division of any advertising agency.

This last is a crucial point, all too often overlooked by enthusiasts for the new generation of Web media. The advertisers and the advertising agencies have invested unthinkably huge sums in their 'traditional' businesses. For many of them, the Internet and World Wide Web is seen not as an opportunity to hone and to exploit new skills and approaches to the creative process, but rather

---

[11] I also wrote that they might well be introduced by means of computer viruses! Fortunately this (as yet) shows no signs of coming to pass.

as a threat that could well undermine the phenomenal income that comes from TV, radio and print-media advertising campaigns. Worse still, of course, is the (false) perception among the product owners that, since the Web is a self-publishing environment, they can devise and operate the advertising campaign themselves.

Given obvious and understandable worries on the part of many advertising professionals about the emergence of the Web, these 'smartverts' are a particularly attractive alternative. Along with these observations there is a parallel one, that the advertising campaign is being cleverly reinforced, particularly in offices that would not normally provide a means – TV or whatever – whereby those advertisements could be seen during the working day!

One area, however, that the advertisers should consider in these smartverts is that of the contractual relationships between the advertisement creators and themselves. For example, if a particular actor has been hired and paid to appear in a commercial, it is worth considering closely whether or not the agreement with them covers the smartvert medium, and whether the licensing for the music, pictures or so forth is sufficiently broad to cover what is still a very new form of dissemination. Intellectual property rights in the context of the Web as a whole are difficult enough; that of PC screensavers is, at the time of writing, wholly uncharted territory. A final thought: what of the owners and operators of the PCs themselves? Are *they* licensed to 'broadcast' the material?

Push broadcasting

At the end of 1996, a wholly novel form of Web-dissemination became available: 'push' broadcasting.* In the normal operation of the Web, users select and download content themselves: their choice of material is entirely their own. Many users, however, visit Web sites and fill out an update form, providing an e-mail address so that they can be regularly informed of any updates to the site, and can then revisit it. Others are frequent visitors to on-line newspapers or other news publications, browsing not the complete set of pages, but only those of relevance to their interests.

Several Web-media producers recognized the importance of this phenomenon: that users like to select their own choice of material – particularly news – but to be informed as often as possible about changes and updates to the material. The notion of 'push' broadcasting was formed, with organizations such as PointCast providing a wide variety of information 'channels' for users to select. An Internet-connected PC is periodically loaded with updated information from the PointCast server. This is not, strictly speaking a 'push', but rather a preprogrammed and regular 'pull' from the PointCast client running in the background on the PC.

When the PC stands idle, instead of a screensaver operating, the PointCast client runs, displaying constantly updated and timely information within a number of distinct windows. In place of an idle computing resource, the user has instead a valuable window on to the world..

And of course – since the service is free of charge to the user – the information and 'broadcast' news tuned for each user and sent to them also includes a continual feed of advertising and commercial-break material. Again, as with the smartvert case above, this fits comfortably with the established practices of the major advertising professionals.

There are of course problems. First, for *home* users there is the unfortunate but all too frequent situation where a poorly configured implementation of the software dials-out from the user's home to the PointCast site so as to update its information resources. This *can* be avoided, with the update only occurring when the user actually voluntarily connects, but even in this case the user could argue that their expensive and limited bandwidth is being 'taken over'. Second, in the *office* case, this bandwidth issue is less of a problem. Here, however, there are other sensitivities, most particularly that the company concerned is, in effect, providing a constantly up-dated newsfeed on to every PointCast-connected user's desk – a service that they would not normally be expected to enjoy! And worse, a service that could well act as a major source of distraction for those workers.

Despite these minor issues, push broadcast shows a strong route forward for the interactive new media, combining the traditional 'pull' elements associated with the freedom of choice familiar to Web users, with a well-focused – indeed, a *self*-focused – choice of news and other information feeds. With the expected rapid progression of digital television – allowing elements of both pull and filtering into what was previously a purely push-medium – we can see two isolated media rapidly and successfully converging. A wider set of facilities will be provided to the end-user, and the advertisers will be provided with a more sophisticated and challenging medium in which to operate, blending traditional *and* new-style skills. In many ways, advertising on the Web might well be seen as little more than practice for the 'real thing' of advertising on interactive, multi-channel pointcast television.

SUMMARY

Although the use of banner advertising has progressed, with many more such advertisers, and with a greater sophistication of banner implementation, they are far from ideal in practice within the Web. Other technological developments have progressed so as to allow advertisers to benefit from a wider range of alternatives – including implementations that are essentially similar to the traditional commercial break, alongside more intelligently and precisely targeted delivery of commercial content through sponsored 'Microsites'.

For any Web advertiser to be successful in the new medium of interactive technology, the most important point to recognize *is* that very interactivity: users – and users alone – choose their navigation route through the maze of Web content, deciding for themselves what content to select and how to respond to advertisers' and to publishers' entreaties. Only the user can therefore decide whether or not even the most carefully placed banner or content link is to be followed, and thereby successful. This progression of user's attention through the Web is driven by the appropriateness of individual content with respect to their (perhaps rapidly evolving) search criteria: every Web user is in fact *looking* for *information* relevant to their interests of the moment.

This might be a part of a research project – formal or informal – or might indeed be a search for particular types of product. Many potentially successful Web advertising programmes have, however, been wasted on the assumptions that a particular user *must* be interested in a given product, simply because the product vendors know that it is (or should be) relevant to them.

For the commercial user of the Web, the 'Eldorado' is the loyalty of a suitable audience – preferably one prepared to pay either for the Web page contents, or for the products and services of their sponsor. For all practical purposes, in the context of the Web this means enticing that audience to visit the commercial Web site of that sponsor – either directly by means of banners or explicit links, or indirectly through further enticements embedded in a Microsite. In both cases the objective remains: to channel visitors towards the sponsor's commercial Web pages.

CORPORATE WEB SITES

6

While sponsored content, Microsites and banners all provide a means of exerting *some* influence over potential customers, by far the most important element of Web advertising lies in the construction and deployment of corporate Web sites. Indeed, all corporate Web sites represent advertising of some kind, since they present an image of the organization to the world.

As we have said, there are over 100,000 such sites, costing their owners anywhere up to $1 million to establish and operate. They range from the simplest of Web-published corporate brochures, through on-line shopping centres, to the most sophisticated, immersive environments providing entertainment, information and even free software. We separate here, however, those 'infotainment' Web sites which act primarily as on-line newspaper or publishing ventures from what are *true* corporate Web sites: pages established, owned and maintained by or for commercial organizations, acting as an on-line shopfront or 'cyberspace' presence. Web-published magazines are using the Internet as a relatively cheap medium for publishing news or other articles throughout the world; by contrast, corporate Web sites seek not to reach a global, on-line *audience*, but rather a set of potential *customers*.

While banners and the rest are of course important –

after all, without these no potential visitor will 'make the link' to the site – the true aim of most if not all Web advertisers is the operation of a successful Web site containing several dozen or even hundred pages. Of course, there are a series of problems to be addressed. First, what does it mean to say that a Web site is 'successful'? Second, how should the site be established and maintained – after all, running a Web site is, for most organizations, peripheral to their main businesses? And third, how can they avoid making the (costly) mistakes that have forced so many of their predecessors from the Web – 40 per cent in both 1995 and 1996 – and that will surely force away many of their cohorts as well?

To answer these problems it is not simply a question of considering the *technical* aspects of establishing and maintaining a Web presence; instead, it is important to examine the way in which Web site and 'traditional' business operations can be interlinked, along with the legal, contractual and operational disciplines of supporting the site itself. That is, far from being a simple technical issue, the Web site becomes a *commercial* issue. This is particularly so because, increasingly, the purely technical considerations are now easily addressed.

Computer companies, ranging from specialist Internet-product vendors, through system and product integrators, to database and general application vendors, all now make available Internet-specific versions of their offerings. Creating Web pages was once a specialist, technical challenge; it is now as easy to achieve in practice as using a wordprocessor or desktop publishing package. In other words, the technology itself is now easily within the capabilities of any technically-competent advertising agency, or even enthusiastic member of an internal marketing team. Technology is *not* the issue; making the content work in a persuasive and commercially viable manner *is*.

TYPES OF CORPORATE WEB SITE

There are many different types of corporate Web site, serving a variety of purposes. At the simplest level, there are Web sites that present the basic information about the company, often in the form of an on-line version of the corporate brochure. Usually, these are 'first generation' Web sites: the organizations concerned established a hurried Web presence: perhaps in response to perceived competitive threats, perhaps out of internal enthusiasm, or perhaps to prevent others registering their preferred domain name. For these Web sites, the pages represent simply a 'quick and dirty' placeholder, or perhaps a toe in the water: they are experimental.

A more evolved form of Web site is similar in overall nature, but in contrast to the reactive site, instead presents a realistic response to a definite requirement. These are the Web sites that contain a variety of information about the company, or that present research papers and other publications that the organization would like to disseminate. In this case, there is a perception that the material itself is of interest, and that it is targeted at an audience that can be expected to have access to the Internet directly. This is a parallel, for example, to the case of many universities or research institutions that make white papers, journal publications or even experimental results available on the Internet.

These two types of site are often confused: or rather, those establishing the former type of site believe that they are copying sites in the latter category. In fact, Web sites that simply present corporate brochure material provide little or no added value, and therefore find it difficult to attract viewers – or at least, to re-attract them after a first, disappointing visit. The key to creating a *potentially successful* Web site lies in attracting an interested audience by providing them with a valuable rea-

son to visit, a compelling reason to stay, and an enticement to return in the future. After all, while a prospect
is viewing *your* Web site, it is certain that he is not
viewing that of your competitors!

In the case of site presenting on-line access to information resources published by the company, the material
is of interest to a certain category of visitors: they might
well have a good reason to come to the site, and can be
counted on to stay within the site long enough to satisfy
their curiosity or research requirements. If the site can
also make clear that the material is updated regularly,
and that a particular series of valuable information items
is shortly to be published (the results of some in-house
conference, photographs of a fashion show, etc) then
there is equally a good reason for the interested visitor
to return.

This continual process of evolving and updating Web
site content is fundamental to the creation of an exciting
and lively set of pages. In the scope of its objectives, such
a site is far more likely to be successful and this of course
leads to a set of good practical advice: publish information about when the site was last modified, what items are
newly introduced, and when a further update is expected.

By contrast, a Web site that simply publishes an on-line
version of their corporate brochures is telling the visitor
what *they* believe the visitor needs to know about *them*.
This is less likely to be of value and, after all, a visitor
interested in that sort of information is able to obtain the
brochure itself. What is more, it is unlikely that such a
site will change often enough – if at all – to justify a
return visit. These sorts of sites are corporate-centric or
brand-centric, not visitor-centric.[12] This leads to the ob-

---

[12] See, for example, Hall, R (1996) 'UK Web advertising comes of age', *.Net*,
December, pp 76–78.

servation of the preferred model for corporate Web sites: in place of an on-line *brochure*, the more successful sites present Web-hosted 'visitor centres'.

The difference in model is readily apparent. Those companies producing a visitor centre (say, for a power station, chocolate factory, etc) realize explicitly that they must attract visitors with things that they, the visitor, will find interesting. Having attracted passing visitors – and realizing that any visit is in fact costing time and money – the company then works hard at justifying the visit: education, entertainment, perhaps even a souvenir shop. For a Web site developed along these lines, the content is planned with the intention of presenting relevant and entertaining information to the visitor and as such, they are more likely to be of interest and of value, particularly given our earlier observation that most if not all Web users are surfing *looking* for information.

Unfortunately, some Web sites can go too far along this approach, presenting not a visitor centre but rather a 'playground' that is in fact essentially frivolous. It is important that the interest and entertainment is carefully balanced by a consideration of the type of visitor required, that is, the type of prospective customer or influencer required. If the site is aimed explicitly at the young, fun-loving user, this playground approach can work well. By contrast, sites aimed at professional users must be more sober, although entertainment can still figure highly.

A further thought, however: as the developer of an entertainment-style Web site, it is worth considering the location from which a user is likely to access the site. Very many Web users access the Internet from a company account. In this case, they are unlikely to welcome overtly frivolous Web pages that might be overlooked by a passing manager!

If the 'visitor centre' model is applied with care, this leads to a description of a third type of Web site: those that are intended to attract and retain an interested audience through content that is deliberately entertaining. While the other two categories might be thought of as 'worthy' sites, these sites act more like the sponsoring of a full magazine or life-style interest publication. Leisure clothing manufacturers, soft drink companies and so forth tend towards these types of site, with an emphasis on providing visitors with amusing games, interesting articles, downloadable screensavers and so forth. Here, there is the perception that the brand name is so well known that the Web site need not try to *sell* it, but can instead be used to *reinforce* it. In some cases, these sites *can* safely become frivolous – such as in the case of youth-market products, for example – but for the more staid brands they are impractical. On the whole, however, these sites represent the epitome of Web presence for many organizations.

There is, however, a fourth type of Web site: the 'hybrid' site. Many of the excellent car manufacturers' sites in particular fall into this category. Here, the sites provide a combination of elements: entertaining games, relevant lifestyle information, useful software, corporate data and so forth. In the case of Vauxhall, for example, this includes access to the TrafficMaster road traffic monitoring systems that are up to the minute, showing possible road hold-ups. They also include details of motor racing news, presentations on new models, screensavers, games and action photography, along with dealer location maps and the more staid, corporate brochure-style detail. In other words, the site provides a little of everything, hoping that the 'scatter-gun' approach will ensure a compelling reason to stay for each category of visitor.

While the entertaining site might well be seen as the epitome of Web advertising, the *true* power of the on-line media only really shines through in this last category of sites. Of course, such compelling, visitor-centric establishments are all the more expensive to maintain but they can be counted on really to add towards the overall brand position of the advertiser.

And of course, for all of these sites there is increasingly now the important opportunity of using the site not merely to present a view of the company's *competence*, but also a means whereby visitors can be supported in actually *buying* goods or services directly, on-line – perhaps within a full-scale, Internet shop. In this case, there are a series of additional concerns that must be addressed, including the question of payment and ordering security. From an *advertising* perspective, however, there is an interesting issue that is particularly pressing: preventing and detecting modifications to the site.

Throughout 1996 and 1997, there have been several reports of Web sites having been modified by hackers: the US Central Intelligence Agency became the 'Central Stupidity Agency'; the UK Labour Party Web pages were altered to replace photographs of the party leader with caricatures. There have been many more, equally trivial examples. However, there have also been cases in which companies advertising on the Web have been prosecuted for displaying erroneous prices – Virgin Atlantic, for example, suffered in this way.

In these cases, the Web page errors were just that: errors. However, it is easy to see that hackers could easily modify prices, order details or even product descriptions on advertising sites, so as to place the company concerned in a poor position. If the change is particularly subtle – unlike the caricatures described above – then it is likely that it will be overlooked. To prevent this – and related problems of fraud and theft of computer-held credit card numbers – it is *vital* that Web advertisers establish suitable security mechanisms. Firewalls, for example, can protect Web servers from illicit access, and Web pages can be protected by the use of sophisticated tools.

Where the pages are carried on an ISP or agency's site, the *technical* detail of ensuring adequate protection will – one hopes! – have been addressed. However, it is important for advertisers to realize that, in law, *they* are responsible for the advertisements. Although the Internet is a new medium, it is still covered by the wide set of advertising (and copyright) regulations. In the UK, for example, the Misleading Advertising laws address the dissemination of advertisements 'in any manner whatsoever'. This certainly therefore covers the World Wide Web!

We can see, however, that there are a broad range of commercial Web sites: from the crudest of on-line brochures, to the most sophisticated of electronic shops, via hybrid entertainment sites. Over 100,000 companies – and several dozen advertising agencies – are busily experimenting and monitoring the various attempts: an exciting and interesting environment.

TECHNOLOGY COUNTS?

Corporate Web sites can therefore be seen to range from the simplest of text or still images – perhaps taking up just a handful of rented pages on an ISP's server – to the most sophisticated of multi-page, multimedia presentations. Within all of these categories of sites, however, there is the ever-present concern of the underlying technology itself. As we have said, for many current or prospective Web advertisers and users, the central issues are *technical* rather than *commercial* – although as we have argued, this should not be the case. The technology itself is of course important but the technology should always be seen as a supporting element of an overall, Web-based marketing programme, rather than as a free-standing and important element in its own right.

At the most obvious level, Web pages can provide support for a range of textual and graphical elements, arranged into combinations of pages. This is indeed the lowest common denominator of Web content. At a more sophisticated level, the Web pages can be subdivided into separate 'frames', or can contain moving graphic elements, embedded applets, 'forms' – interfaces for allowing correspondence – and 'beneath' these pages, the Web servers can set and manipulate the cookies we discussed above. It is possible to achieve subtle and incredibly powerful effects with the most technologically competent Web pages – but is this really, truly necessary?

An important issue to consider is that of the *viewer*: while these technologically impressive pages might well represent the optimal Internet-programming capabilities of the Web page designers; it is still necessary for the viewer to be able to retrieve and benefit from them. Extensive use of high-resolution or moving graphics, for example, undoubtably provides viewers with interesting and intricate Web pages. However, if the user is connected via a telephone link and modem to the Web server, it might well take a long, long time to download these pages. In this case, if the page graphics add decoration but no *real* value, who can blame the viewer for interrupting the transfer, and perhaps then visiting a rival page?

It is of course understandable that Web page designers would wish to use complex and interesting graphics and layouts, after all, in the 'traditional' world of advertising, such techniques are a stock in trade for attracting attention. However, while the Web does indeed support many interesting possibilities for such pages, it equally penalizes advertisers for their clumsy application. That is not to say that such complex pages do not have a place in the Web: they clearly do, but only as appropriate. For example, while complex pages might be too time-consuming for the *home* user, they might well be appropriate for those accessing the Internet via a corporate local area network (LAN). If the primary audience for a given page or site is *those* users, the use of complex graphics and other technologies might well be justified.

The important points are therefore not related to the use of particular technologies, but instead the use of *appropriate* ones – where appropriate is considered with respect to the objective of the Web site and the intended audience. The Web site is a part of an ongoing and broader marketing programme; it must fit into that programme, rather than be an excuse for demonstrating competence in Java programming and HTML design.

GETTING IT RIGHT!

There are a large number of ways in which corporate Web site projects can go wrong. As the previous section discussed, developers can succumb to the temptation to use excessive and inappropriate graphics or applets, for example. Or worse, the site can be made publicly accessible while it is still 'under construction', or with parts that do not work as advertised: links that go nowhere, graphics that fail to load, etc. All of these errors are the Internet equivalents of poor store management: no owner of a large department store or supermarket would *dream* of opening without all elements of the establishment being in place!

Rather than concentrate on the ways in which sites can go wrong, however, in this section we shall examine the ways in which they can *work* and thereby, hopefully, succeed in satisfying the commercial requirements placed on them. First and perhaps most obviously, the technical elements of the Web site should be appropriately chosen for their audience, and care must be taken to ensure that they operate effectively. For most Web sites, a so-called 'Webmaster' will be appointed, and part of their job should be the ongoing maintenance of the site: ensuring that all links connect to the required destination, that graphics load correctly, and that the pages are of a consistent style. Usually, it is advisable for the Webmaster periodically to access the site from a connection equivalent to those provided for the site's primary audience, ie via a slow modem link or fast LAN connection as required. It is also advisable for the Webmaster to be tasked with checking that those pages have not been *modified* either accidentally or by hackers.

Beyond these practical considerations, it is of course important to understand what the site is expected to achieve. It might be used, for example, to present key information resources, entertainment messages, or an element such as free software. These must all be carefully placed within the site. The analogy would be with real-world shops, where substantial research into shoppers' habits has led to a detailed understanding of the best ways of creating an effective store layout. Shoppers, for example, are enticed deeper into shops by placing so-called 'destination items' close to the back wall, and with impulse purchase items close to the checkout tills.

While equivalent research has yet to be undertaken in the realm of *virtual* shops, there are still some analogies that can be drawn. For example, some parts of the Web site will correspond to the destination item – perhaps through external or banner advertising alerting prospects to the availability of a new screensaver, game or picture. While these *can* be placed deeply it is unlikely

ADVERTISING ON THE INTERNET

that visitors will have the patience to browse through several pages to reach them – after all, unlike the real-world shop, they cannot in fact actually *see* them on the 'back wall'. What is more, assuming that they do go to the deeper pages, part of the site's objective is to encourage repeat attendance but on subsequent visits they might well simply record (that is, 'bookmark') the destination page itself, thereby bypassing the intended route through the other sets of commercial messages and content.

However, placing destination items in the first screen is equally a mistake: visitors will simply view or collect the information and then rapidly leave. What is required is a balance, tempting the visitor deeper into the site with items of interest and the encouragement to move on to further pages – all the while presenting them with the information, messages and persuasion that the site is intended to deliver.

Another common aspect of amateur Web sites is the provision of a set of links into other, equally interesting Web sites. While this is appropriate for an enthusiast site, it is far from appropriate in a commercial arena: unless the link is to a co-sponsor or close partner – from whom the visitor can be linked back to your site – external links should be used sparingly. After all, the objective of the Web is to attract and to retain visitors: simply letting them leave at the earliest opportunity is a waste of their interest in your site, and reduces the opportunity to influence them further.

Assuming that the Web pages are created and maintained in such a way as to retain a viewer's attention, the Web site can only then really succeed if it can achieve the primary, advertising objective: the *influencing* of the viewer – and this can only be achieved through a developing dialogue. It is important to recognize, however, that this influence needs to be carefully co-ordinated with the existing corporate marketing and sales approach. For example, it is possible through a Web site to provide a prospect with the most comprehensive and complete view of the company's offer. A view so complete, in fact, that the prospect can decide for him- or herself that the goods or service are not appropriate. If, however, the old-fashioned sales approach of a conversation with a knowledgeable – and of course persuasive – salesperson was used, the prospect might well have come to realize that a slight adaptation to the product or service *would* have been ideal. The Web site could *lose* a sale.

Of course, for catalogue sales or the equivalent, the Web site is ideal in the simplest form. In other cases, the developers must work hard to ensure that the dialogue is sufficient to whet an appetite without exceeding the basic commercial requirements.

Finally, for the commercial, Web-based dialogue to succeed, clearly it is necessary for the Web site to 'know' about the prospect – his or her requirements, preferences and so forth. This can be achieved by targeting a generic prospect – or better still by the dynamic tuning of Web content driven by cookie analysis, as discussed above – based on the prospect's pattern of attention through the Web site itself or through partner Web sites with whom such profile information is exchanged. Of course, as discussed above, this analysis must be carefully performed so as not to impinge on the prospect's rights of privacy, but if done with sensitivity – and the prospect's knowledge and consent – this can be an ideal means of ensuring that the prospect *and* advertiser benefit from the visit.

VANITY PUBLISHING

Perhaps the most important aspect of the development of corporate Web sites lies in the question of the publishing medium itself. For many Web users – be they newcomers or part of the old and established set of Internet 'netizens' – the fundamentally attractive feature of the network is its support for self-publishing: at heart, the Internet grew up as an amateur's medium, attracting the hobbyist publisher. Any simple exploration of Web sites rapidly produces a wide range of home-grown home pages, owned and operated by students and enthusiasts. Of course, not all sites are operated by unpaid amateurs: some are owned and operated by professional publishers, by advertising agencies, and by marketing executives within large corporations. An important point to recognize, however, is that even these are essentially run by *amateurs*.

The Web is a new medium. It is only a few years old and just like the early days of television, and indeed the early days of *printing*, those displaying material are learning their business. In large and small corporations, it is still the case that the establishment of a Web presence owes much more to enthusiastic individuals than it does to the hard-headed assessment of accountants and business managers. Gradually, however, this is changing driven by growing experience, by the perception of an increased role for on-line commerce (discussed in the next chapter) and by the rapid deployment of Web expertise in the advertising and related industries.

It is, however, certainly the case that – as a DIY environment – the Web can be used by enthusiastic amateurs to publish corporate information and content around the world. Indeed, for some organizations, this was their only realistic, initial alternative, particularly given that their existing advertising agencies might not have had in-house resource to help them. Is this amateur approach now a mistake? It is.

The Web site must *work* – not just technically, but as a key part of the ongoing marketing programme. As such, it is important that the Web material supports – reinforces – the existing brand images and brand evolution. Web content is important but equally, for commercial users, so too is the commercial operation of the site. The Web pages must fit into the existing selling process, without undermining it; the Web image and 'personality' must be chosen in such a way as to work alongside ancillary but very important items such as the existing corporate brochures, trade exhibition boards and even sponsored events. We have said that putting just a corporate brochure on-line *is* a mistake but so too is creating a set of Web pages with a different 'look and feel' to that brochure. The key here is 'media integration': these distinct elements must be interlinked so that they reference, support and are maintained alongside one another.

It is of course possible to achieve this media integration without using the same source for each element but it becomes a more difficult task. And as the technical issues are now easily resolvable, the problems of establishing and maintaining a successful Web site become increasingly commercial or branding problems. DIY and hobbyist sites are of course sufficient for the hobbyist, seeking to tell the world cheaply about his or her family, friends and pet; for the *commercial* Web site operator, the business deserves – and indeed, *depends on* – a more professional approach than this.

SUMMARY

In summary, the initial key questions of this chapter can be reiterated:

▶ What does 'success' mean in the context of a corporate Web site?

▶ How are the corporate Web sites to be established and maintained?

▶ How can the owners and operators of those Web sites avoid the costly mistakes of their predecessors?

First, 'success' can only really be attained by reference to the core advertising purpose: increased sales. Of course, the advertising – since it is there to support the marketing programme as a whole – might achieve this objective by alerting consumers to a change of brand image, by reminding an audience of its existence, by reinforcing a well-known brand, or by simply presenting attractive prices for a product and inviting sales. All of these have the opportunity to be 'successful' – but only where they fit the marketing programme.

To adjudicate a Web advertisement – banner, Microsite or corporate Web site – as being successful, it is therefore necessary to have an understanding of the overall objectives. Of course, in the case of many corporate Web sites there are further advantages in this assessment: primarily, the high measurability of Web-based activity. If, for example, an on-line purchase is made within a company's Web site then clearly the advertisement has been a 'success'. To date, however, most purchasing has taken place outside the Web environment, although as we shall see, this is rapidly changing. Measurement in this case is more problematic, and so additional procedures are required within the existing purchasing and order satisfaction processes. Again, this points back to the need for the Web and 'real-world' marketing aspects to be closely integrated.

To summarize, 'success' is determined relative to the *commercial objective* of the complete programme into which the Web fits.

Second, as we have argued, the corporate Web site *can* be maintained by the company itself. Better, however, is to use professional assistance – and preferably with some integration with the rest of the marketing programme. It is no surprise to find that the most successful of the Web advertisers tend to use the same – albeit, *large* – agencies for both traditional and on-line advertising tasks.

Unless the company concerned has in-house expertise, it is also better to use the services of professional agencies or ISPs to support not just the development of the Web site content, but also to provide the ongoing maintenance and support of the site. This is particularly important when the *visibility* of the site is considered. A Web page is potentially viewable throughout the world, 24-hours a day. Because of this, it is important that the Web site host system is equally available continually and, moreover, that adequate security measures are in place to protect the Web page contents from accidents, hackers or 'digital vandals'.

Where the Web site is hosted by an ISP or professional partner, the responsibility for this support becomes theirs and, what is more, if the system *fails* then the company injured by the advertising loss can obtain compensation. If the site is developed and maintained internally, the company certainly has greater *control* over the system and pages but equally, it has a greater *responsibility* for them.

Third, the only way in which *any* advertiser can avoid repeating mistakes is of course to be aware of those very mistakes themselves. Other Web advertisers have failed primarily because they have been unable to attract a reliable flow of visitors to their sites and have been unable to convert into prospects those visitors that *have* come. That is, Web advertisers fail for exactly the same reasons that traditional-media advertisers fail. This should be heartening: I have assumed that you already know how to advertise in the regular print or broadcast media. There is no 'royal road' and so there are no hidden pot-holes!

The keys to Web advertising therefore are:

► define the ideal market and assess how closely the Web-available audience fits that ideal;

► understand the elements of Web interactivity that might appeal to that audience – in particular remembering that Web users crave information more than simple entertainment;

► place suitably imaginative banners within content that would attract that audience, and ensure that Microsites or sponsored content are available to them; and

► make sure that the Web site itself is established in such a way as to retain the audience's interest, with material that is refreshed often enough to encourage repeat visits.

THE **FUTURE** OF
ON-LINE SHOPPING

7

Advertising on the Web has quite clearly now become a major part of our modern commercial environment; and as we move towards new and more advanced interactive media, such as on-demand digital television, it will become ever more important. It is unrealistic to expect that, with the increasing reliance on *commercial* support for the infrastructure of the 'global information superhighway', it will not be heavily used to deliver intelligently focused and effective advertising messages.

As we have said, however, advertising exists to support key marketing programmes – and these in turn exist to increase sales. Wherever more *advertising* takes place within the new media, it is hardly surprising that there is a parallel interest in satisfying sales requests equally on-line. Internet shopping and World Wide Web-supported electronic commerce are therefore an important and fast growing aspect of the modern commercial environment.

There are many reasons why this should be so. For the companies involved, a globally-accessible Web site is more cost-effective than opening a worldwide network of high street shops. For the *customers*, Web sites offer convenience in shopping hours; and by being able to compare prices in shops around the world, the buyer can also ensure a good deal. If there are any worried parties in this equation it is the *taxation* authorities, concerned with the very real prospect of an invisible and essentially untrackable pattern of expenditure – and perhaps even of earnings with the growth of electronic money.

Electronic commerce is already a big business. IDC, for example, put the e-commerce market at $3 billion for 1996, although Forrester Research quote a more modest $1.3 billion, based on a slightly different view of what constitutes such commerce. Both, however, are roughly agreed on the rapid increase in this figure that the next few years will bring, with IDC projecting that 2000 will see a market of $100 billion, while Forrester figures are around $95 billion. Clearly, observers expect a fundamental shift in buying and trading habits at the end of this century.

Perhaps the most important observation to make, however, in the context of electronic *commerce* is that it is far from limited to the issue of on-line *shopping*. Businesses can trade one with another, and banks can provide a means for performing transactions on-line. In the case of banks, this is particularly attractive: a Booz Allen & Hamilton survey in 1996 showed that the average cost of an Internet bank transaction was just 13 cents, versus over $1 for a high street branch transaction. In all fairness, however, the Web-based advertising is primarily aimed at the individual consumer, and so it is the private shopper on the Internet that will interest us here.

The key question with regards to on-line shopping, however, is this: are the Web users *shoppers* or are they on-line *buyers*? At least initially, it was expected that the users would fall into the first category. This is a reasonable expectation – after all, as we have observed above,

Web users are primarily searching for *information*. However, beyond this they are also users of computers and of computer software – and equally, the manufacturers and vendors of software in particular have learnt to take advantage of the World Wide Web. A wide range of software is now bought over the Internet and many software developers, particularly of games, have learned to make limited versions of programs available for free, encouraging users to experiment before purchase.

As well as software, mail-order of CDs has also been an important early aspect of on-line shopping. Music CDs in the UK typically cost the same amount in sterling as the same CDs cost in dollars in the US. Given the exchange rate, this means that CDs bought in the US and delivered to the UK – even allowing for the delivery charges – are still very much cheaper. No surprise then that Web users are enthusiastic purchasers of CDs via on-line shops. Similarly, books and flowers are purchased on-line – and for different reasons, so too is pornography.

At present, software, CDs and flowers amount to around 52 per cent of on-line purchases and travel a further 24 per cent, according to Forrester Research, whose survey projections show such on-line *shopping* growing in value to a staggering $6.5 billion by 2000. KPMG in fact suggest that as much as one in five of UK sales will take place over the Internet by 2001.[13] Clearly there is an expectation that many of these on-line shoppers will become on-line *buyers*.

In the case of software, flowers and CDs, however, there are clear reasons why consumers are willing to purchase

---

[13] From the *Computer Business Review*, 9 January 1997.

on-line: either because they are already used to buying such goods remotely, in the case of flowers say; or because the prices make it a particularly attractive option in the case of software and CDs. For on-line shopping and electronic commerce to *really* take off, there are two further types of purchase that must be enabled: regularly bought, physical goods such as *groceries*; and equally regularly bought but intangible goods such as *information*.

In both cases, we are of course seeing rapid progress. In the UK, for example, several leading supermarkets have begun experiments at providing an on-line shopping facility to allow customers living within delivery range of certain large superstores (such as the North London Tesco, for example) to buy on-line. Customers receive specifically tailored software that includes details on the current range and prices. From this, off-line, they create an order, selecting groceries and other items as required. When they access the superstore, the prices and goods are updated, and the total price is presented. If the customer wishes, they can then buy the selection with a credit or loyalty card and have the shopping delivered at a time of their choice.

Although experimental at present, all reports agree that (despite some teething problems) this is an effective and very convenient shopping style.

By contrast, the on-line payment for information is not yet fully established. In this case, instead of the normal free access to a Web page containing, say, an electronic newspaper, visitors will instead be expected to pay. There *are* some paid-for sites on the Web at present: some of the 'adult' sites; and access to professional information services, for example. In this case, the payment model is through a 'membership' scheme, with the visitor presenting a user/account name and password.

As this develops, however, publishers are exploring the prospect of demanding payment of a small sum – a so-called 'micropayment' – on entry. Small means around the 10 cent mark, or in some experiments, as low as 0.1 cents.

While the facility for payment through accounts or from a credit card are now being slowly put in place, parallel support for micropayments is still at the experimental stage. For on-line shopping to become a more fundamental aspect of our daily lives, however, it is clear that this technology is very important. This is particularly so given the perceived high levels of concern over the basic *security* of on-line shopping, whether through the use of pre-established accounts, credit cards or the newly developed digital cash.

These have all, however, been addressed in the last two years. For basic, secure communication Netscape developed the SSL standard. This allows browsers to access Web pages and to provide information – such as order or private data – in such a way that it cannot be intercepted. Clever hackers *have* managed to break the encryption codes in some cases: this is not perfect – but then again, there are risks on the ordinary high street, and users seem increasingly willing to accept the risks on the information superhighway.

This has been bolstered by the rapid development of secure communication technologies acceptable to the credit card companies and banks. On 30 December 1996, the first transaction using the new 'Secure Electronic Transaction' (SET) standard was undertaken by Master-Card. This is important because, until the development of SET, the credit card companies perceived the Internet as a risky environment and were not prepared to permit *any* transactions through it.

Finally, DigiCash, Mondex, VISA and many others have begun to make electronic cash systems available, allowing much smaller transactions to be supported. This last promises to have the greatest impact, allowing payment for much smaller items – an individual Web page, for example – to be supported.

SSL has reached the status of being effectively now an Internet standard; SET is likely to become the standard for credit card transactions. There is as yet no clear favourite for electronic cash, although it is widely expected that such a standard will develop through 1997. Because of these, the secure base for on-line shopping is essentially now present. What has been missing until now is the *confidence* of Web users in applying these technologies despite the fact that Web shopping is by no means less secure than 'traditional' mechanisms, and is in many cases far *more* secure.

1997 has been heralded by many[14] as the year in which electronic-commerce, digital cash and on-line banking will all become a realistic and viable part of our economy and of our everyday lives. If this is so, then Internet advertising will continue to grow in importance, and will continue to develop in technical sophistication and in creative imagination.

As we have said throughout the text, there is nothing 'magical' in using the Internet and World Wide Web to support commercial messages – the pervasive myths notwithstanding. The advertising regulations apply as equally to the Web as to a newspaper; similarly, the basics of good headlines and effective copy apply in the new medium. The only difference – and it is a *big* one – is that the medium is interactive. Never forget: the Web

---

[14] See, for example, Stibb, D (1996) 'The birth of digital commerce', *Fortune*, 6 December: 'In 1997 consumers will start living up to their name on the Internet'.

audience is only a click away from you and can escape your clutches as easily. Encourage them; entice them; perhaps even *lure* them – but never take their attention for granted!

Advertising on the Internet is relatively cheap, covers a widespread audience, and provides the exciting opportunities of exploring a new and interactive medium. Good luck.

INDEX